BOBBY ON THE BEAT

Bob Dixon spent years "on the beat" as a police constable with the Metropolitan Police in the early 1960s, witnessing all manner of incidents, from the serious to the ludicrous. Spending the majority of his time in London's East End dealing with drunks, fatalities on the road, domestic disputes, and even suicides, as well as policing at major public events such as Guy Fawkes night, New Year's Eve, and anti-Vietnam War marches, life was colourful and varied, if not always safe. This memoir of a London copper charts Bob Dixon's experiences as a young police officer before he joined the CID, covering his life before signing up for the force, his rigorous training, and the vagaries of first patrolling the beat, as well as the lighter side of policing.

BOBBY ON THE BEAT

MEMOIRS OF A LONDON POLICEMAN IN THE 1960s

BOB DIXON

LARGE
PRINT

First published in Great Britain 2013
by
Michael O'Mara Books Limited

First Isis Edition
published 2015
by arrangement with
Michael O'Mara Books Limited

A catalogue record for this book is available
from the British Library.

ISBN 978–1–78541–085–7 (hb)
ISBN 978–1–78541–091–8 (pb)

Published by
F. A. Thorpe (Publishing)
Anstey, Leicestershire

Set by Words & Graphics Ltd.
Anstey, Leicestershire
Printed and bound in Great Britain by
T. J. International Ltd., Padstow, Cornwall

This book is printed on acid-free paper

For Anne, Steve, Andy, Chris and Tina

Contents

Contents

Preface

The Metropolitan Police was formed in 1829 on the instructions of Sir Robert Peel, the Home Secretary, who appointed Sir Richard Mayne as the first Commissioner.

When I joined in 1961, on the very first day at training school all recruits had to learn the words written by Sir Richard and we were tested on them the next day. Those words which were imprinted on every constable's mind stated the definition of an efficient police, and I think are worth repeating here. Sir Richard Mayne wrote:

> The primary object of an efficient police is the prevention of crime; next that of detection and punishment of offenders if crime is committed. To these ends all efforts of police must be directed. The protection of life and property, the preservation of public tranquillity, and all absence of crime, will alone prove whether those efforts have been successful and whether the objects for which the police were appointed have been attained.

A very profound statement, which I believe is as relevant today as it was in 1829, or 1961 when I had to learn it off by heart. I understand that the Met no longer instil it into recruits, as the curriculum is now designed for all forces in England and Wales. It's a pity, as I think all officers could do well to remember Sir Richard Mayne's words when performing their duties.

Introduction

The police force of the 1960s and 70s was somewhat different than the one we know today. It is difficult for those who did not live during that era to comprehend exactly what life was like in those days. Certain aspects of our everyday existence were still influenced by the aftermath of the Second World War, some food rationing had only just finished, there was no internet technology or forensics and the public had a totally different outlook on life.

Some of us who are old enough may remember watching the 1950s film *The Blue Lamp* and the television series *Dixon of Dock Green*, which ran between 1955 and 1976. Both were about the fictitious Police Constable George Dixon, played by Jack Warner, and his exploits patrolling his beat in the East End of London. Dixon was portrayed as the loveable beat copper, friendly, experienced, sympathetic and understanding, but firm with the local villains. I worked with just two or three "George Dixons" during my time, and I've known a few older folk who still believe that all police work during that era was as portrayed in the series. Some of it was and I hope in this book I convey that, however, it would be wrong to view everything from those days through rose-tinted glasses. I have tried as far as possible to tell it as it was, warts and all.

I have attempted through my experiences to paint a picture of life in the East End of London, the inhabitants who lived there, particularly the cockneys, and their relationship and attitude to the local police officers who were part of their community. The 1960s was described as the era of free love and flower-power, but most of the folk living in the East End of London were far too busy struggling for a better life and future to be part of that.

I joined the police in 1961 and served for fifteen years. This book covers a period of about ten years when I served in areas that included Limehouse, Bethnal Green, Bow, Arbour Square and Leman Street, as a uniformed "bobby on the beat" and in plain clothes prior to joining the CID.

I have been totally honest in my writing, perhaps a little too honest at times, but I felt it important to relate events as they happened. Some readers may be shocked at certain revelations about how we dealt with situations. However, I would ask that you don't compare police procedures and practices in my day with those of today.

I have attempted to paint a picture of the excitement, sadness, humour and fun, all of which were part of everyday life for the bobby on the beat in those days. Every case and incident I describe actually happened and I have tried to recall each to the best of my ability. I have changed the names of most characters — villains and police officers — including mine, also in some cases locations, purely to protect the guilty, including me!

Perhaps I should dedicate this book, in part at least, to dear old George Dixon.

CHAPTER
ONE

Why the Police?

I was the first member of my family to join the police. I came from a very happy, stable and loving family background. My father was a merchant seaman, my mother a schoolteacher, and I have a brother and sister. I don't really know what drew me to wanting to become a copper but perhaps it might be that despite my happy childhood, and the great times I had at school, I was always fascinated by the totally different world of cops and robbers.

We lived in Southampton, I attended the excellent King Edward VI School and, from the age of about fifteen, I often went to the local magistrates' court during the holidays to listen to cases. I was interested to see and hear a side of life alien to my cosy existence — the burglars, cheats, liars, drunks and violent characters who appeared each day, and of course to see the victims of the perpetrators. I also very much admired the eloquence of some of the lawyers — their use of the English language. My grandfather and mother were schoolteachers and I was quite interested in the possibility of entering that profession. However, I became particularly interested in dealing with young people in trouble and thought the probation service might be my vocation.

I arranged a meeting with the chief probation officer in Southampton but he informed me that I could not apply for that job until I was twenty-three. He advised me to go and get some experience of the world. I told him that as an alternative to eventually becoming a probation officer I was thinking of applying to join the police. He said, rather prophetically, that if I became a police officer I would never want to join the probation service; that turned out to be true.

Yes, my mind was made up, on leaving school in July 1959 at the age of seventeen I would join the Metropolitan Police Cadets. However, I found I had to wait until I was eighteen to enter the cadets, and so for a couple of months I washed cars at a local garage to earn a few pounds. Little did I know that because of that short hiatus my life would change completely and I would very quickly grow from a typical teenager into a man. At the time, a friend of mine was looking for work and I went with him to the local youth employment office. While he was being interviewed I saw on the noticeboard that a government research ship, the *John Biscoe*, was shortly sailing to Antarctica and was recruiting crew for a two-year contract. What a fantastic opportunity! I decided the Met Police could wait awhile and I would join them later not as a cadet but as a constable.

Four weeks later there I was, just eighteen and only recently left school, experiencing the delights of the

7

bars and houses of ill repute in Montevideo, South America, from which I am happy to report I came away unscathed. I had been accepted as the youngest member of the thirty-two-man crew, which comprised mostly of very experienced seamen and several scientists. We'd sailed from Southampton in October 1959.

Two weeks after Montevideo I was in Port Stanley in the Falkland Islands, and a week later witnessing the amazing scenery of Antarctica, including the icebergs, penguins and seals. Finally, in January 1960, having forced our way through the pack ice of the Weddell Sea, we arrived at Halley Bay, 800 miles from the South Pole and the first British ship to go there since Sir Ernest Shackleton in 1915.

Between 1959 and 1961 I completed two voyages south on *John Biscoe*. I didn't realize it at the time, but I learned so much that would later stand me in good stead, not only to deal with situations in the police but in everyday life. Living in a small close-knit community on board ship, sometimes in difficult conditions, can be quite testing. A person who is usually a good friend can suddenly get on one's nerves for some trivial reason. We rarely talked about our own problems, yet it was so important that we all got on and tolerated each other. Those two years taught me to gradually understand another person's point of view, to listen to others' opinions and, most of all, not pre-judge a situation. I put much of this into practice later when confronted with very difficult situations involving people I met as a bobby on the beat in the East End of London. I doubt that I would have learned that much in the police cadets.

On arriving back in the UK in 1961 I immediately applied to join the Metropolitan Police. Why the Met, apart from the lure of London? The truth was, nobody else would have me! I wanted to join Southampton City Police or Brighton Police but they required giants of five-foot-ten and above, they would not consider dwarfs of five-foot-eight like me. The Met was the only option.

The selection process was pretty quick. Personal checks were done about my background and testimonies were given by my next-door neighbours and friends in Southampton. I attended the recruiting centre in Borough High Street, South London. There were about twenty applicants. The first part of the process was the medical, the nature of which was surprising.

First my height was checked and eyesight tested. At that time anyone who had to permanently wear glasses was disqualified from joining — that does not apply today and the height requirement has also been reduced. Three applicants failed the eyesight test. Tattoos on a candidate were only acceptable if they were not visible when in uniform. I had none, although I later worked with a colleague whose hobby was being tattooed. His body was covered in them but not one was visible when he was wearing uniform. One applicant failed as he had tattoos on his fingers.

Next we were required to undergo a medical examination, which I found quite bizarre. After being told to strip and put a towel around our waists we were informed that an experienced doctor would examine us and that he was simply looking to make a decision as to whether we would be fit to serve twenty-five or thirty years. I stood on a mat in front of the doctor, he asked me to drop the towel and walk across the room and back, turn around, bend over and touch my toes, turn back to face him and stand on one leg then the other. Next he looked in my ears and mouth. That was about it. I don't even remember him listening to my heart, surely he did? I assume medical records were provided by my GP, but I had expected a much more stringent examination.

After we had all been examined we were told if we had passed or not. Of the sixteen applicants who took the medical test, eight failed. One in particular was not happy and voiced his opinion in no uncertain terms, and perhaps he had a point because he was a well-known professional boxer who was about to fight for the British and European titles and considered himself pretty fit — he subsequently won the titles.

Next came the written examination and I was one of three applicants who were exempt from taking it because of the O and A levels I had attained at school. Of the five who sat the exam, four passed to join us three for the final part of the selection process — the interview.

The panel comprised three senior officers and it was much as I expected. Apart from them asking the usual questions such as, "Why do you want to join the Metropolitan Police?" — receiving the standard answer,

"To help other people, have an exciting life and a rewarding job" — they spent most of the time asking me about the time I had spent in Antarctica. I had quite an easy ride. After the interviews, three of us were informed that, subject to reference checks, we had been passed.

A few days later the letter arrived at home, confirming my successful application and instructing me to report to Peel House Training School in London. I was delighted and my parents were so proud of me.

CHAPTER
TWO

Peel House — Initial Training

My life changed on 8 August 1961. I was just nineteen years old and about to be appointed a constable in the Metropolitan Police. I arrived at Victoria Station in London from my home in Southampton and walked to Regency Street, where I reported for training at Peel House. At that time, the Met had two training centres, Peel House and Hendon. The former, named after the first Commissioner Sir Robert Peel, was an old Victorian building that was first used by the police in 1907, when four weeks' training was deemed sufficient. Hendon Training School was opened in 1934, and at the same time the training increased to thirteen weeks, which is what I undertook. Now, the course lasts for twenty-six weeks. Peel House closed in 1968.

My first impression of the place was that it reminded me a little of pictures I had seen of the German prisoner-of-war-camp Colditz Castle, with a courtyard surrounded on three sides by tall, grey buildings. The courtyard was used for the daily morning parades, marching drills, dealing with mock-up traffic accidents and the like, and the buildings comprised classrooms, a gymnasium, the canteen, lecture rooms, a library, a television lounge and dormitories. The latter were small, partitioned single rooms with a bed and desk; also there were communal washrooms and showers. When recruits started their training they were in Class 13, and each week the class number reduced until the final week when they became the exalted Class 1.

In the armed services I know that initiation ceremonies are carried out on new recruits. At Peel House we did not experience this although, on returning to our rooms on the first night there, several of us found that recruits from Class 1 had removed our beds and piled them up in the washrooms. It took us about an hour to sort that out.

There were twelve recruits in our class at Peel House. We came from varied backgrounds, the military, one was unemployed, there was also an ex-public schoolboy and a police cadet, among others. Our class instructor was a sergeant, who lectured us on a number of subjects, while other lectures were given by different officers of various ranks.

After becoming acquainted with each other and our surroundings on that first day, we were given bookwork to learn in the evening, the first subject being "The primary object of an efficient police", which we were tested on the next morning and had to be word perfect. This was to give us a taste of what was to come. Apart from the physical part of our training, a vast amount of it comprised of very intense learning during the day and in the evenings. As well as daily tests, we had four exams each week, failure of which meant being "back classed" for one week. We all helped and tested each other with our learning and luckily nobody suffered that ignominy.

The next day we were taken by coach to Great Scotland Yard, then the headquarters of the Met, which was situated on the north Embankment of the Thames. I had seen the world-famous building many times in films and on television and it is difficult to explain my feelings as I entered. I was awed by the vast history of this building, and excited by the part I was to play in it. We were directed to a small room where we took an oath, swore our allegiance to Her Majesty the Queen and were welcomed as Constables in the Force by an assistant commissioner. To say I was proud is an understatement.

We were then given a tour of most of the building. We saw the information and control room, which dealt with all emergency calls and was in constant contact with police cars on the streets of London. Next, we were taken to the fingerprint and photographic departments, where our fingerprints and photographs were taken for official records. The criminal records office was most interesting. It contained the records of all persons charged with crimes, detailing the nature of them and the outcome of their cases. We were not shown the Black Museum, which displays many items and exhibits from famous crimes — possibly some of them were thought too macabre for new recruits to see at the start of their careers.

Our final stop that second day was to the uniform store in South London, where we were completely fitted out with winter, summer and ceremonial uniforms including greatcoats, capes, gloves, helmets and boots. Loaded up with our newly acquired wardrobes, we returned to Peel House for a well-deserved dinner — the food was always plentiful and good. We had been told that we had to prepare our uniforms ready to appear on the parade ground the following morning after breakfast with the rest of the school. Our evening was spent ironing shirts, brushing tunics and particularly polishing boots. The latter was a complete art, only accomplished by a couple of ex-Army lads in our class who seemed to get the required results on the first evening, the rest of us took most of the thirteen weeks, despite the military instructions they gave us.

Needless to say, the morning parade proved a complete shambles for Class 13, who had not yet been given any marching or parade instruction. Although discipline was strict and expected standards high, in general the "bull" we encountered during our training was nothing compared with what one could expect in HM Forces — however, we were ripped to pieces for our turn out on that first parade and I think every one of us was ordered to get a haircut later that day with the visiting barber.

Into lessons, and the first task was to elect a class captain; we chose the oldest member of our group who was in his early thirties, an ex-Marine married with two children. The decision was unanimous and he was a

15

good leader and popular. As with any group of lads, we had several real characters in the class. One was a Londoner, cockney through and through, an amateur wrestler and a comedian who frequently had us all in fits of laughter, including the PE instructor in the gym during the self-defence lessons.

Although our class started with twelve recruits it wasn't long before it sadly was reduced to eleven. One night, after another evening of intense study for us all, we went to bed and settled down for the night. Suddenly, at about 1 a.m. we were woken by shouting and screaming coming from one of the dormitory rooms. We rushed to see what was happening and found one of our colleagues putting on his uniform and screaming that he was going out to kill people. He was throwing himself about, foaming at the mouth and barking like a dog. Although we often went out for a drink after our studying, none of us had been out that night. The night-duty sergeant was quickly on the scene and told us to hold him down on his bed, which it took five of us to do, he was so strong. He continued to fit, scream and foam at the mouth but very soon a doctor arrived and gave the poor lad an injection that sedated him prior to being taken to hospital.

The next morning, our class was in sombre mood when we were informed that our mate had suffered some sort of brain malfunction that caused him to fit, and that he would not be returning to us. The prognosis was that he probably would not be able to have any future employment that would cause him stress or overtax his brain. We felt so sorry for him and our class captain wrote a letter to his parents on our behalf, conveying our feelings and wishing him all the best. We never heard what happened to him.

Our training continued at a relentless pace but we still managed to have a few beers at the local pub, the White Swan, affectionately known by us all as the Mucky Duck. Being based in Victoria, unlike the recruits in training out at Hendon, we had been warned not to be tempted by the bright lights of the London's West End. However, the warning fell on deaf ears and on one or two occasions several of us found ourselves wandering "Up West" — most had not previously sampled London life and this was the start of the swinging sixties. We were supposed to be back in Peel House by 11p.m. when the doors were locked. Any dirty stop-outs would get in by climbing a small drainpipe up to a first floor window of the dormitory, which was always left slightly open for the purpose.

After the first two weeks we were allowed home every week from lunchtime on Saturday until 8a.m. on Monday. I went home some weekends to see my family and friends but remained at Peel House for others. My wage was £13 per week and even then train fares were quite expensive.

When the exams approached we all revised like mad and somehow managed to pass, although we were constantly told we were the worst class to pass through Peel House — I wonder how many others heard that?

The curriculum was extremely varied and very interesting. We were required to learn a great deal of

English Law, criminal law as well as Common Law, Powers of Arrest, Traffic and Licensed Premises Regulations, among others. These subjects were taught by lectures and book learning but also with a great deal of roll-play and demonstrations. Some of the lectures were longer than others and the one on "How to Stop a Runaway Horse" was as follows: "Run in the same direction as the horse and pray."

We received a small amount of instruction on Civil Defence training and I recall the instructor saying: "You will know if there has been a nuclear attack. You will hear a fucking great bang!" We were lectured on such things as the intensity of fallout from radiation dust, how to measure the radiation dosage of roentgens per hour and how selected police officers would be taken to the country, away from the nuclear blast, and then return in mobilized columns to clear up the mess. All good stuff no doubt, but it was a subject about which I had little comprehension or interest. A year or so later, in view of the Cuba crisis and the build up to the Cold War, more detailed instruction was given to recruits. Senior officers were given specific instructions to carry out in the event of a nuclear attack but luckily they have not yet had to be put into practice. I'm afraid anything to do with nuclear fallout went straight over my head, if you'll pardon the pun, and as far as I'm concerned what will be, will be.

All classes paraded each morning for inspection. As the weeks went by regular drilling by the legendary drill sergeant, an ex-boxer affectionately known as Punchy, honed our skills noticeably. I remember one particular drill session with amusement. It was a warm day and we were not wearing our uniform tunics, just trousers and shirts.

"Eft-Right-Eft-Right-Halt!" yelled Punchy. He marched up to me and screamed "Constable, what the bloody hell is that sticking out of your back pocket?"

"It's a biro, Sergeant."

"I can see it's a fucking biro and if you don't remove it pretty quick I will ram it right up your arse!"

Muffled laughter followed from the rest of the class.

Punchy picked on me on another occasion when a bus went past the parade ground. "Did you like that bus, Constable?" he enquired.

"Not particularly, Sergeant," I replied.

"Don't look at the bloody thing then and pay attention to my sodding instructions."

The Parade ground was also used to teach us traffic control, which was quite hilarious. One recruit was supposed to stand in the middle of the square, conducting traffic at a road junction. The rest of the class acted as traffic — one representing a car, two for a lorry and three for a bus — and as I recall we only had one lesson in this highly skilled activity. Because of the much bigger area at Hendon Training School, they had roads marked out, pedestrian crossings, junctions and traffic lights; we had to improvise. I was later to spend hours conducting traffic at one of London's busiest road junctions and I can honestly say that my training at Peel House in the art of directing traffic was absolutely useless. I sometimes think the instructors only included it as a laugh.

On one occasion during a lecture, without any prior warning, a "character" ran into the classroom screaming and shouting, fired a pistol, pushed the lecturer to the floor and ran out. The lecture continued as before, much to our bewilderment, but after about ten minutes we were told to give a written statement of the incident, including a full description of the assailant. The recruits then read out their statements and it was amazing how much they differed, particularly as to the person's description, including their hair colour and height. Some said he was wearing a hat when in fact he wasn't. The object of the exercise was to show how unreliable witness statements can be and to teach us not to rely solely on them.

Fitness was important and we spent time in the gym becoming proficient at self-defence. Also, we were given instruction in how to use a truncheon, should it be necessary, the main point being to use it on the arms and legs and not the head.

We were all required to pass a first-aid examination and to show that we were reasonable swimmers. Life saving was optional but most of us volunteered and went to the swimming pool at Hendon Training School for the test, part of which was to retrieve a brick from the bottom of the pool while wearing clothing. We had been told to bring our pyjamas for this. When the time came for us to don our night attire, you can imagine the reaction of the recruits and the instructor when the cockney comedian of the class appeared in a pink diaphanous baby doll nightie . . .

On Wednesday afternoons we were taken to Hendon for sport. We were more or less allowed a free choice of which activity we participated in; I chose rugby, others football, basketball or swimming. I represented Peel House in the annual Met Police Rugby Sevens and although we did not win, we gave a good account of ourselves.

Our training was very professional and we had lectures on famous murders, firearms, suicides, fingerprints, scenes of crime — DNA had not been discovered then — which were given by senior officers and experts in their field. We were shown numerous photographs and exhibits relating to those subjects. We also visited a mortuary, which I found fascinating. We watched a pathologist carry out a post-mortem on an old woman who, it transpired, had died from natural causes. None of us had seen a post-mortem before and the pathologist explained in detail exactly what he was doing and the functions of the various organs of the body. One of the recruits felt sick and had to leave the room, but the rest of us seemed unaffected. Later in my service I attended a number of PMs and was privileged to watch the renowned Home Office pathologist Professor Francis Camps at work in two murder cases.

One of the first things we learned was what approach to take in any incident, such as a road accident, a pub fight or a domestic dispute. We were instructed to first enquire, "What has happened here, Sir, please?", which seemed very polite. When dealing with a road accident the instruction was always to approach and deal with it as follows: Casualties (Is anyone hurt?), Obstruction (Is the accident causing an obstruction that can be dealt with?), Witnesses (Did anyone see what happened?), a sequence that was known to us all as COW.

Old cars, motorbikes and cycles were used for mock accidents, the instructors would act as victims and witnesses and we all had to roleplay as the police officer dealing with the incident. On one particular day, it was the turn of probably the most shy and quiet recruit in our class. He approached the mayhem in front of him and, as taught, enquired, "What has happened here, Sir, please?" He was informed by the instructor/witness that a car had gone out of control and hit two others. The recruit stood more or less frozen to the spot and speechless, his nerves seemingly having taken over. The instructor watched our embarrassed mate for what seemed ages. Nothing.

"Well, Officer?"

Nothing.

"Cow, C. O. W. you idiot!" yelled the instructor.

"Oh yes, Sergeant, sorry, I forgot. Are there any cows injured?"

Everybody fell about in hysterics. I am certain that our colleague's response was not deliberate but the result of pure nerves, which anyone who has been required to do roleplay will understand. We all were picked on at various times but thinking on our feet was a great way to quickly instil us with confidence.

I was embarrassed one day on the parade square when dealing with an accident. I carried out the correct

COW procedure and ascertained that there was one injured person who needed hospital treatment. In the corner of the square was a phone box, and the instructor ordered me to go to the box and call for an ambulance — and to use a loud voice so that the observing class could hear what I was saying. Everyone knew that it was not a working phone box but just used for roleplay, however I did as instructed. "This is Police Constable Dixon. Can I please have an ambulance at Peel House, Victoria; I have one male person injured in a road accident. Thank you."

"What did they say?" the instructor asked me, although of course the line had been dead.

"They said an ambulance will be along in a minute."

I went back to continue to deal with the casualty, and you can imagine my shock when I heard the ringing bell of an ambulance on an emergency call approaching. Suddenly, an ambulance screeched through the gates of Peel House, blue lights flashing, bell ringing, and on to the Parade Ground. Two crew jumped out at the accident scene, asked me what had happened and took control of the casualty. Full marks to Peel House for their reality training. It had been well planned and culminated in a first-aid talk and an insight of what ambulance crews expect from police officers at the scenes of accidents.

I was later told by a woman police officer I met, who trained at Hendon, of an incident she experienced while there. During a lecture, she was leaning forward on her desk with her arms folded. The instructor yelled at her, "Miss, will you kindly get your fucking tits off your desk!" The shocked WPC burst into tears and walked out of the lecture. She was instructed to report to a senior officer who, although showing her some sympathy, explained that the incident was nothing compared to what she might encounter when she left training school and was required to break up a pub fight on a Saturday night — when tears would definitely be out of the question. The WPC accepted the reason for her admonition. Evidently, that sort of incident was quite common at the time with the female recruits, to see how they would react.

One thing that really bugged the instructors when we were doing arrest roleplay was the habit most of us had of saying to the offender, "I'm afraid I am going to have to arrest you," or "I'm sorry, I am going to have to arrest you." It was hammered into us, "You are *not* bloody afraid or sorry about anything, you are a copper for Christ's sake!" We got out of the habit by the end of the training.

There was a mock-up court, with a witness box and dock and this was one part of the training that I loved. This probably stemmed from my love of the English language and the times I had spent listening to cases at Southampton Magistrates' Court prior to joining the police.

Giving evidence in court was a part of police work that I thoroughly enjoyed throughout my service and I testified in most categories, including juvenile, magistrates' sessions, the central criminal court known as the Old Bailey, the appeal court and coroners' courts. I never

tired of listening to eloquent lawyers, who mostly had great knowledge of the law and command of our language, presenting cases or examining witnesses. The greatest barrister I ever encountered later in my career was in a murder case at the Old Bailey, when I was cross-examined by Mr Quintin Hogg, later to become Lord Hailsham and Lord High Chancellor. He was brilliant, but I like to think I gave as good as I got in our exchanges.

Time seemed to pass so quickly at Peel House and suddenly we were Class 1. The final exam was looming and most evenings were spent revising and testing each other on all we had learned. I did not go home for the last three weekends and spent them with my girlfriend of the time, revising. She was very helpful testing me, and in the end probably knew as much about the Road Traffic Act Construction and Use Regulations as I did. I also remember one Sunday afternoon, after having a boozy pub lunch, going back to her flat, lying on the bed together for a relaxing few hours and trying to revise the Sexual Offences Act 1956. This dealt with among other subjects rape, unlawful sexual intercourse, indecent assault, indecent exposure, prostitution and brothel keeping. She must have liked me.

We all passed the final exam and were looking forward to seven days' leave, but first there was some celebrating to do. There was no Passing Out Parade, as there is today, but we all went out for a huge drink and meal in the West End near Trafalgar Square. Two of our instructors, an inspector and a sergeant, joined us and we paid for them. We got fairly drunk but did not

disgrace ourselves or the police force. We were all aware of what we had achieved and were proud of ourselves. However, one amusing incident did occur when we arrived back at Peel House.

One of the lads went to bed feeling the worst for wear. After a short time he went to the toilet and started what can only be described as projectile vomiting in a bright red colour. On seeing this, he started shouting for help and the more sober of us went to his aid. He was convinced he was having a stomach haemorrhage. I then remembered that this clown had spent the whole evening getting drunk on vodka and tomato juice and when I pointed this out he calmed down, went back to bed and slept it off. Everyone to their own taste, I guess.

After seven days of well-deserved rest at home in Southampton, I returned with my class colleagues to Peel House to hear where my posting was going to be. The Met's area at that time was split into four districts within Greater London, which comprised of approximately twenty-two divisions, each of which had various numbers of police stations. As our names were read out, we were given our warrant card, which was official proof that we were now constables in the Metropolitan Police.

I waited in anticipation, wondering where I was going to be a bobby on the beat. The West End perhaps, posh up-market Kensington, West London near London Airport or would it be out in the sticks in some leafy suburb?

The inspector read out my name: "Ah, Constable, I hope you're ready for this. This'll keep you busy. You're going to keep the 'salt of the earth' in order in the East End. You are going to Limehouse, Chinatown, on H Division."

I can honestly say I was delighted, and I wondered what the coming years would hold in store for me.

One other lad in my class also received the same posting and later that day we were taken, together with all our uniform, to Limehouse Police Station on West India Dock Road, in the heart of London's East End.

Although Peel House was an old building and was in its last few years of being used as police training centre, I certainly benefited from my thirteen weeks there. However, my life as a London "copper" in the real world was about to begin.

CHAPTER
THREE

Joining Division

After leaving Peel House for the last time, having said goodbye to my nine colleagues who had been through the enjoyable hell we had shared for the past thirteen weeks — and most of whom I would never see again — I was taken to H Division headquarters at Arbour Square in Stepney. There, I was given the extra tools to carry out my job, known as appointments. They comprised such things as a truncheon, torch and whistle and chain with a key to the street police boxes. I only ever used my whistle once during my time in uniform: several of us were chasing a suspected thief through a block of flats and temporarily lost him, but on seeing him hiding behind a wall I blew my whistle to alert my colleagues and the suspect was arrested.

I was also issued with a blue-and-white striped armband to be worn on the left wrist of my uniform when on duty and removed when not — I never quite understood the thinking behind that because I couldn't see a constable, in uniform and on his way to work, not being approached by a member of the public because they had recognized that he was correctly not wearing his armband and therefore off duty. I guess it was just a tradition, and it was eventually dispensed with in 1972. We were not provided with handcuffs, which were available at police stations, if required, but were not carried by the beat bobby as they are today. Finally, I was given my individual divisional number, which had to be worn on epaulettes at all times for the purpose of official identification.

The Metropolitan Police area was split into divisions, and each division had several police stations. H Division stations included Arbour Square, Bethnal Green (the home of the notorious Kray family), Bow, Isle of Dogs, Leman Street (where I was told the records of the Jack the Ripper murders were still kept, although I never saw them), Limehouse and Poplar. Although an officer was posted to a particular station and would carry out most of his duty there, he would at times be sent to another station if extra personnel were required for some particular reason. During my time in uniform I carried out duties at all stations on H Division for odd days.

I finally arrived at Limehouse Police Station in West India Dock Road. It was a large, fairly modern-looking building comprising of a front office with access for the public; a communications room manned at all times by a civilian and a constable, giving connection to and from street police boxes, all other stations and police cars; and also a charge room, a medical examination room, an interview room, about ten individual prisoners' cells, and a larger one used to accommodate several prisoners. On the first floor were the CID offices and other administration offices. At the rear of the building was a large canteen and there was also a yard and a garage for police cars and the van. The latter was a vehicle with an area in the back that was big enough to transport three or four prisoners and was often referred to by the public as a Black Maria. The origin of the name comes from the 1830s and refers to a large black woman named Maria Lee, who owned a lodging house in Boston, Massachusetts, and who assisted the police in ejecting drunks from her establishment and getting them to the police cells.

Adjacent to the police station was the section house, where all single officers lived — affectionately called by some the "sexual house", although it never lived up to that name, as female friends were not officially allowed in our rooms. I later learned that rules were a little more lax in other smaller section houses around London ... Our section house was named Harold Scott House, after a previous commissioner, and housed officers from all stations on the division. I lived there from when I joined in 1961 until my marriage in 1964, and spent a very happy time with my friends and colleagues. One big advantage of residing there was that on "Early Turn" there was no travelling to work, one simply had to fall out of bed and arrive at the adjacent nick, perhaps a little bleary eyed.

In the early 1960s the London docks were still probably the busiest in the world. Along the River Thames, from Tilbury to the East and West India Docks, ships came from all parts of the world and their crews naturally comprised all nationalities, colours and creeds. The pubs, restaurants and prostitutes of Limehouse played host to them, giving the police the problems one might expect from drunken sailors on shore leave with pockets full of money and often unable to speak the language. I had empathy with some of the merchant sailors — after all, I had been staggering around drunk in South America not all that long ago (I was actually arrested in Montevideo, but that's another story . . .).

The indigenous population of Limehouse, Stepney and the surrounding areas were made up of large numbers of dock workers and they regarded themselves as the real East Enders, the genuine cockneys, having been born within the sound of Bow Bells. In Mile End, the Jewish community, many of whom had fled Europe under the Nazi regime, were very much involved in the rag trade, owning numerous garment-producing factories. There was also a large Polish community, and the West Indian immigrants had just started to arrive in the UK and begun to settle in the East End.

Limehouse was known as Chinatown and there were numerous Chinese restaurants in the area. Although they kept very much to themselves we had a lot of dealings with the Chinese, particularly on a Friday and Saturday night when their restaurants attracted many customers who might be the worse for wear. There were also a few Indian restaurants around at that time.

Each of the Limehouse beats had numerous public houses, which varied from the typical family pub, where there was always a knees-up and sing-song on a Saturday night, to the very popular East End entertainment pub, with drag acts and comedians. One

31

particular large pub, the Eastern, situated at the junction of West India Dock Road and East India Dock Road, was frequented by sailors and prostitutes. However, although there were pubs which were mainly patronized by those who today we would call gay, that scene was nowhere near as open as it is now, in fact the word "gay" was not even used, and such folk were still known as homosexuals and often more derogatory terms.

Considering the variety of pubs and their clientele in our area, the pubs presented surprisingly few problems and I think that was due mainly to the licensees. We had a good rapport with them and they were able to sort out most troubles without having to call for the police, but they also knew they could rely on us for support. Remember, these were tough times and we're talking about tough people — they did not require the bouncers and security staff we see today.

One particular very notorious and popular pub situated a few yards from West India Dock gate was called Charlie Brown's, named after a previous landlord. It was a real spit-and-sawdust pub, quite literally, and was frequented by a very varied mixture of customers including sailors, dockers, prostitutes, transvestites and cross-dressers. It was said that if you asked any sailor anywhere in the world where to meet when in London, Charlie Brown's was always the answer. In 1944 a member of the bar staff had been stabbed and killed in the pub by an American sailor. Sometimes it was difficult to tell who was male and who was female among the clientele and it only became apparent when they entered the toilet marked either Male or Female. In addition, on most weekend evenings well-known personalities from the world of entertainment and sport would visit, prior to enjoying a meal at a local Chinese restaurant. Frank Sinatra and Judy Garland visited when in London. Apart from the history, the attraction of the pub was, quite simply, the landlord, a legend in his own lifetime, Billy Vincent. He was an amazing character who I eventually got to know fairly well. He presented himself as one character behind the bar but quite another when not. During opening hours, Billy was larger than life, and at times very rude to most of his customers, who loved his humour. When serving a drink he would often ask, "What the fuck do you want?" and when the pub was closing he would shout over the microphone, "I've had your money, now all fuck off home!"

But after closing time Billy would invite a few of his friends, including off-duty Old Bill, to stay for a lock-in. He was a different person then, even quite shy and at times morose when talking about his past life. He was a most generous person and one Christmas gave me presents for my wife and son. Although a friend to the police, he never expected or asked for any favours and was not given any.

One summer I was on holiday with my family on a boat on the Norfolk Broads when another tourist boat came past us quite close. Suddenly, I heard a booming voice coming across the water from the other boat, "Hello there, you bloody big tart!" It was Billy Vincent, who was on a day trip with other publicans and had spotted me. I replied in a likewise fashion, goodness knows what everyone in earshot must have thought.

These were some of the diverse characters at Limehouse who I was about to start to get to know and respect, and whose life and safety I hoped I would be responsible for in some small way.

My first two weeks were spent at Thames Magistrates' Court in Stepney, just listening and observing court procedure. The court was the local one, which dealt with cases from all police stations on H Division, and the one I would be attending frequently following arrests that I had made. It was presided over by a stipendiary magistrate who was a trained lawyer, whereas some courts are attended by lay magistrates. Thames was an extremely busy court and each morning a conveyor belt of prisoners who had been arrested the night before for things like being drunk and disorderly would file in to receive summary justice, usually a small fine. It was common to see about thirty such prisoners per day. They would be followed by prisoners charged with more serious offences, some of whom elected for a trial by jury or who were sent to a higher court because of the serious nature of their offence. The afternoons in court were mainly spent dealing with traffic offences.

Duties at Limehouse, as at all London police stations, consisted of three shifts: Early Turn 6a.m. to 2p.m., Late Turn 2p.m. to 10p.m. and Night Duty 10p.m. to 6a.m. Each shift was worked in three-week cycles and the main duty on each was primarily beat patrol, although times of day would dictate some activities, such as school crossing patrols.

The relief, as each shift was known, collected in the parade room fifteen minutes prior to the shift starting and was first inspected by the duty station sergeant and inspector. Next, we had to "show our appointments", which meant producing our truncheons, whistles and report books, which were required for recording incidents, including road accidents. We were then given general information regarding crimes such as burglaries that had taken place and any details appertaining to our particular beat of which we needed to be aware.

There were six beats and one officer would be allocated to each. The beats were varied and presented the officer with different challenges — some were mainly residential areas with large blocks of flats, some covered the dock areas and huge warehouses along Regents Canal, others covered the shopping areas and two smaller but busy beats covered the Chinese restaurants and popular pub areas. One particular beat was interesting in that it included the aptly named Narrow Street, a labyrinth of dark alleyways and overhead walkways that connected tall, imposing warehouses on either side. In the eighteenth and nineteenth centuries, ships from all parts of the world delivered their cargoes to the warehouses, including tea, coffee, sugar, rum, silks and furs, and in the 1960s some of those goods, such as wine, wood, paper and spices, were still being imported. It was a pleasure to patrol Narrow Street and to smell those beautiful aromatic spices and chat with the stevedores who unloaded the ships. At night it was pretty much deserted and could appear rather eerie, with silhouettes of the huge cranes on the dockside looming in the darkness above the warehouses and wharfs.

A little further along the Thames was Wapping, on H Division but just off the Limehouse beats, a dock area steeped in history. One could visit the execution dock at Wapping Old Stairs where between the fifteenth and nineteenth centuries, pirates were brought to be executed in public and their bodies thrown into the River Thames, the most famous being Captain Kidd in 1701. During the 1960s, Wapping was made famous as the supposed home of that outrageous fictitious East End character Alf Garnett from *Til Death Us Do Part*. In fact, he was supposed to live on Garnet Street, which is still there today.

Each Limehouse beat covered an average of about three to four square miles and apart from walking around the area, dealing with any incident that might arise, being observant and using his initiative, an officer would be expected to get to know the public and business people who lived and worked on his patch.

In addition to the six beat officers, the relief also had: the van driver; the communications officer, who would be posted for three weeks in the communications room; a reserve officer, who would assist with front officer duties; the station sergeant who was responsible for the running of the station, including dealing with prisoners; a sergeant, who would assist him and also go out on patrol to check up on the beat officers; and the inspector, who was fully responsible for the relief.

On the early and late shifts a constable would be posted to traffic point duty at one of the busiest road junctions in London, the Eastern, so called because it was immediately opposite the big pub of that name. Five roads converged on the junction, including East and West India Dock Roads and Commercial Road, which all carried the vast numbers of huge lorries, travelling to and from the various London docks. The constable would be stationed in the middle of the junction and did his best to keep the traffic flowing smoothly. That posting lasted for the full three weeks and was hated by all of us.

There were two women police officers at Limehouse, who did street patrol and dealt mainly with juvenile offenders and victims. Dog handlers were not attached to a relief but were available when required and were often called upon. The CID worked separately from the uniform branch but liaised with us when we arrested anyone for a serious criminal offence.

So here I was, fully trained, my court attachment completed, kitted out as required with an immaculate uniform and shiny boots, and ready to be let loose on the citizens of Limehouse. Well no, not quite, my superiors didn't have the confidence I had in myself, not just yet anyway! I was required to spend three weeks walking the beats with other officers in order, not to just learn the geography of them, but to be shown the ropes. Those weeks proved invaluable for learning the real world of policing. I was paired up with a different officer each day on Early Turn, Late Turn and

Night, so I quickly got to know all my colleagues, who made me very welcome.

The lads were quite a varied bunch. Some were much older than me, ex-military and very experienced officers who had been at Limehouse for many years, others were my age, early twenties with little experience. Some were married with families and lived away from Limehouse; others were single and like me lived in the section house. We all seemed to get on well together as a team both on and off duty.

On my first day I was paired with an experienced officer named Dave who had come from the RAF and been at Limehouse for several years. We were posted to 3 Beat, which was the busiest of the six. It was a cold, crisp November morning and still dark. Having just turned six o'clock, the streets were busy with people making their way to work and large numbers of them were men going to the West India Docks. In the 1960s their union was strong and one stevedore later told me that getting work in the London Docks was virtually impossible unless you had other family members working there. Positions were more or less passed down from father to son.

"Right, the first thing is a nice cuppa," explained Dave, "And we get that from the garage in Commercial Road, which should be open by now."

A couple of minutes later, we were sitting in the garage manager's office, drinking mugs of hot tea and making general friendly conversation. He seemed genuinely pleased to see us and handed Dave a piece of paper with the description of a driver and car that had

38

filled up with petrol and driven off without paying the day before. Dave said he would pass the details on to the CID. After ten minutes we were back on our beat and walking at a slow pace around the extremities.

"OK, Bob, what did they teach you at training school?"

"The same as they taught you I suppose, Dave. The basics that we would need to perform OK out on the streets."

"I suppose you got 'What has happened here, Sir, please?' "

"Yes, but I'm not sure how that will work here in the East End."

"It won't, mate, it's a load of old bollocks. You try going into Charlie Brown's or the Eastern at chucking out time on a Saturday night and sorting out a punch up with a load of pissed-up dockers and sailors and saying that to them, they'll tell you to fuck off in no uncertain terms."

"What would you say, Dave?"

"Oh, I would just tell the governor to turn the music off, hit the bar with my truncheon, then shout at the top of my voice 'OK, you bastards. Pack it in or I'll call for the cavalry and we'll nick the lot of you.' That usually works — and you'll find the locals and regulars in the boozers don't want aggro and will back you up."

One had to be generally polite when dealing with members of the public, of course, but that was the end of "What has happened here, Sir, please?" as far as I was concerned!

The Eastern Junction Traffic Point was on 3 Beat, and Dave explained that the poor bugger who was directing traffic there every day for three weeks, for eight hours a day except for his forty-minute meal break, was entitled to an unofficial ten minutes tea, fag and comfort break. The PC on 3 Beat would normally give him those breaks every couple of hours. We went to the junction and I watched as Dave went to the middle to relieve our colleague. The changeover was an art in itself as the traffic was extremely heavy and had to be kept flowing. Dave stood behind his mate, took the white armlets from him and put them on, at the same time keeping up the sequence of traffic flow. (Any resemblance to running around the square at Peel House pretending to be cars and lorries was purely coincidental!)

There is a saying that if you see a huge traffic hold-up there is nearly always a policeman causing it. I am afraid, perhaps embarrassed, to admit that it may be true — certainly during my time at Limehouse, on occasions, it was. All of us hated the traffic point duty posting and although it was important to concentrate on what one was doing, it could be quite boring, particularly if the traffic flow was light. In order to liven things up a little, two or three officers were known to deliberately cause a traffic problem by giving one road a longer run than the others, creating a tailback for the latter. This would then create a problem for the officer to sort out, which would take quite a few minutes. It was also not unusual when arriving at the traffic point on the changeover from Early Turn to Late Turn to find your colleague was handing over such a situation for you to deal with. Generally though, I doubt our actions caused much addition to the traffic problems that were always evident in and around the London Docks area.

The fumes from the vehicles were horrendous, and at the end of the shift our clothes and faces would be filthy. Although the Clean Air Act had come into force in 1958, smog, a toxic mixture of fog and smoke, was still a problem during some winter months. In December 1962, London was covered in thick smog that caused problems not just for travel but also to the health particularly of the elderly. The conditions lasted for four days, during which over 700 people died from respiratory problems. I remember that period very well as I assisted with controlling the traffic flow at the Eastern Traffic Point. It was virtually impossible to see beyond about six feet in front of you, and although the government had advised the public to wear breathing masks if going out, we were not issued with any. The smog was choking and we tied handkerchiefs and scarves around our faces. Officers were stationed at the junction of all five roads and although we had our torches they hardly penetrated the smog. To get vehicles, mostly of which were heavy lorries, across the junction we simply shouted instructions to each other and walked in front of the vehicles waving a torch. The smog drifted and lifted slightly for short periods, enabling the vehicles to move on very slowly once we had directed them over the junction.

One Saturday I was on Late Turn and posted to the Eastern Traffic Point. It was about 2.45p.m. and I was standing in the centre of the junction waving my arms about, thinking about nothing in particular except keeping the traffic flowing, which was fairly light, it being a Saturday. I signalled a coach to proceed across the junction but the driver stopped in the middle and leaned out of his window to speak to me.

The coach was full of football supporters from Sheffield and the driver asked me if I would direct him to Millwall Football Ground, where United were playing in the FA cup, the kick-off being at 3p.m. Millwall is located on the Isle of Dogs, about a mile from Limehouse and well signposted, which the coach driver had obviously been following. The problem was that Millwall Football Club did not, and still does not, play their matches on the Isle of Dogs but south of the River Thames near the Elephant and Castle and Old Kent Road, several miles from Limehouse. I informed the horrified driver and directed him to go via the Blackwall Tunnel — there is no way he would have got to the ground in time for the kick-off and I sometimes wonder, knowing the impatience of football supporters, what the atmosphere in that coach was when they learned the reality of the situation.

During my three weeks of learning beats I soon became familiar with the practices that would make patrolling a little easier in the future. The first thing I was told to learn was the location of basement laundries and boiler rooms, under certain blocks of flats, which were never locked. They were always warm and provided a great bolthole in the middle of long, freezing, wet winter nights. It was not unusual to take refuge from the elements for a few minutes and meet up with a mate from an adjacent beat for a chat, exchange of information and a fag. I suppose some might consider such conduct time wasting or skiving, but the blocks of flats and their walkways were such labyrinths that criminal damage and other crimes were common, so they would often be visited by PCs anyway.

Another popular port of call on one of the beats during the night was a biscuit factory. We would pop in for a chat, a cup of tea and a biscuit with the night workers, who would often give us a large bag of broken biscuits for the staff back at Limehouse nick. Sometimes they would also give anyone who had kids a bag as well.

Two of the Limehouse beats were quite a way from the station and patrolling officers were expected to phone in twice during their eight-hour shift from a police box to report that all was well with them. Most of the six beat officers would return to the station twice during their shift for ten minutes for a coffee, also for a forty-minute meal break. However, an officer on one of the outer beats could, if he wished, take his breaks in a police box. The box was exactly as depicted in the television series *Doctor Who*, which started in 1963. Inside there was a stool and small desk and it had a phone linked directly to Limehouse police station, to which the public had access. If the station wanted to contact the patrolling officer or a police car, a blue flashing light on top of the box would be activated.

I was advised that, should I decide at any time to take my refreshments in the police box, it would be best to eat them at one sitting and not leave any to return to later as it was not uncommon for a greedy colleague from an adjacent beat to visit the box and devour any food that might be there. I also spent the early weeks on division getting to know various publicans, Chinese and Indian restaurant and cafe owners, shopkeepers and local business proprietors. The vast majority were always glad to see the beat constable and cups of tea or coffee were frequently on offer.

I found the Chinese very interesting folk, quite reserved and polite. Chinatown, of course, made famous by stories of Sherlock Holmes, Fu-Manchu and opium dens, has a great history. The Chinese first came and settled in Limehouse from the Far East in the late 1800s, the locality being close to the docks to which the trading ships came, opium being a part of that trade. Most of Chinatown was obliterated by Nazi bombing during the Second World War, as was Limehouse, after which Chinatown moved to Soho in the West End of London. However, in the 1960s, there was still a thriving community in Limehouse. I am sure opium played a part in their lives, but I was never aware of it. Limehouse's Chinatown was also referred to on stage in the old time music halls, firstly by Gertrude Lawrence in 1921 in the song "Limehouse Blues", and later in 1932 by George Formby in his comic song about Mr Wu called "Chinese Laundry Blues".

I very soon realized that the Chinese were not people to cross or upset. One particular evening while patrolling, my attention was drawn by a taxi driver to a disturbance a short distance away in West India Dock Road. He told me that he'd seen men fighting with machetes. I hurried to the scene where I saw three waiters from a nearby Chinese restaurant chasing a man round two taxis parked on a taxi rank in the middle of the road. One waiter was waving a machete above his head and the other a baseball bat. I shouted at them to stop, which they immediately did and they told me that they were chasing the man, who appeared the worse for drink, because he had run from their restaurant without paying.

By this time, two of my colleagues had arrived in the police van and I could, of course, have arrested both waiters for possessing offensive weapons — the man for running off without paying his bill. I decided to use common sense instead and offered all parties a compromise — the bill to be paid, as he had sufficient money, and the waiters not to be charged — to which they all agreed. I would not normally have suggested such action if someone was running around the street threatening others with a machete and a baseball bat but I felt on that occasion it was justified. I knew such incidents involving the Chinese and non-paying customers were not uncommon, and although we would warn the restaurant proprietor against such actions, one could understand why it happened. I never knew of any such weapons being used to inflict injury on anyone, which would, of course, have resulted in arrests.

Such actions can also backfire and result in unforeseen and serious consequences, as the owner of a Chinese restaurant in Whitechapel was to find out. In 1968, when serving in the CID at Leman Street, I dealt with a case that occurred at a restaurant in the Whitechapel Road. It started in similar circumstances to the one above, with a customer decamping at around 11p.m. without paying for his meal. He was chased by waiters, not carrying weapons, who threatened him and made him pay. About two hours later, with the restaurant full of customers, a group of seven men, armed with an assortment of weapons — including baseball bats, lengths of wood and hammers — burst into the premises and completely smashed it up. The petrified staff and customers took refuge in the kitchen and under tables. Uniformed officers quickly arrived but the attackers had fled. Next morning, I was deputed to carry out the investigation and it did not take me long to arrest the man who had attempted to run off without paying for his food. I subsequently arrested five others and all were charged with causing a riot (a fairly rare charge), assault and criminal damage. All were sentenced to terms of imprisonment.

I wonder if the public ever question why the police helmet is shaped as it is? I found out the answer very early on. When we were on Night Duty and it was time for a refreshment break and some of us fancied a Chinese meal, one of us would go to the back door of our favourite restaurant, which was very close to the nick, and order our choices of delicious oriental food;

nothing too runny though and definitely not soup. The chef wrapped the meals very thoroughly and they would be placed in the helmet, which would then carefully be put on the head. This was in the days before takeaway food was widely available and it was not thought a good idea for an on-duty policeman to be seen carrying a Chinese meal up the road in the early hours of the morning. Therefore, a careful, slow, short walk back to the nick with the chow mein tucked neatly under the helmet seemed the obvious solution. We always paid for the meals but occasionally were given a discount for being good regular customers. We also carried out the same operation with fish, chips and curry.

Sometimes, when not on duty, I would visit a cafe called The Greasy Spoon near the West India Dock Gate. It was frequented mainly by dock workers and I can honestly say it served up the best full English breakfast I have ever had. It was also interesting listening to the dockers using their typical industrial language to discuss their work, world problems and West Ham United Football Club.

One particular transport cafe on Commercial Road, Limehouse, was Bill Mayes Transport Cafe. It was used by numerous lorry drivers to break their journeys to and from the docks. There was officially no parking allowed on the very busy Commercial Road, and the beat officer was specifically instructed to make sure that lorry drivers did not stop for any length of time in the vicinity of the cafe. One or two officers seemed to take a great delight in booking and prosecuting drivers for parking offences without giving them any warning. (This was in the days before traffic wardens and parking tickets.) I always thought such swift action was unfair and I preferred to go into the cafe, tell the drivers to be quick, finish their tea and bacon sandwiches and move their vehicles. I never had one driver take advantage of the situation and I never booked any of them.

Reporting members of the public for traffic offences was not a favourite of mine — some of my colleagues seemed to love it and they would often transfer to the traffic division to specialize at the end of their probationary period. I obviously did report for summons anyone committing what I considered serious traffic offences, such as jumping red traffic lights, parking within the restrictions of a pedestrian crossing, etc. I was usually fairly lenient with any driver whose road tax was just out of date, although that was often a sign that they had no driving licence or insurance. The latter was a definite booking offence as far as I was concerned, and my pet hate because of the possible consequences it could lead to.

Contrary to popular belief we were not given target figures to achieve for stopping suspects, arrests or traffic violations. It wasn't necessary as there was always plenty of action going on in each of those areas, however, as every constable was on probation for two years and his work constantly monitored, if he was not performing his duties as expected he would be given advice as to how to improve.

From the beginning of my time on the beat I dealt with various types of road accidents, some serious and involving pedestrians. One particular accident from my early days, which made an impression on me, occurred on a pedestrian crossing. A little boy aged five years, on his way home from school, ran on to the crossing to meet his mum who was waiting on the other side. He was hit by a lorry which was not travelling fast but just had no time to stop.

The poor boy's foot was completely crushed under a front wheel and one can imagine the horrific anguish the mother suffered witnessing it. I was close to the scene and immediately took control. An ambulance arrived very quickly and I remember having to pick up the little lad's boot which contained part of his foot and handing it to one of the ambulance crew. The lad was taken to Poplar Hospital where his foot was amputated.

There were several school crossings on the Limehouse beats, most were patrolled by civilian lollypop ladies but, when they were not able to do so, the constable on the particular beat had to perform the duty in the morning, lunchtime and afternoon. I did not relish that duty, much as I appreciated the opportunity to project the image of the friendly policeman to the young kids.

When learning beats I was advised by an older officer to wear gloves when doing school crossing duty because some of the "little darlings" would ask to hold your hand while waiting to cross the road and you could end up with a fistful of very sticky sweets or even worse. The duty did have a couple of benefits though; first, kids would give us Christmas Cards, sweets or something they had made at school and, second, I never objected to chatting with some of the young mums.

One colleague I worked with, Pete, was a very funny character who suggested to the lads on the relief that we should play a game of finding the most obscure offence being committed by a member of the public. Most of those offences were usually to be found in the Road Traffic Act, Construction and Use Regulations and consisted of such things as a vehicle having dirty headlights or a number plate not being the correct colour. If a constable submitted a report of one of those types of offences the station sergeant was not too pleased and the reported person would usually receive a written warning instead of a summons. Pete always seemed to want to test the patience of the station sergeant and his ambition was to report someone for an offence on a par with unlawfully driving sheep across London Bridge, beating or shaking a rug, carpet or mat in the street, flying a kite or, my favourite, a taxi driver not producing his bale of hay when requested to do so, which proved that he was committing an act of cruelty to his horse. All these offences had been on the statute books for several hundred years — and some still are, however, taxi drivers can relax as the requirement to carry hay was repealed in 1976.

Pete never gave up though. One evening at about 7p.m., we were on Late Turn and although it was not quite the official lighting-up time the light was fading. I suddenly noticed a horse pulling an open cart along

West India Dock Road, an unusual sight to say the least. I then could not believe my eyes when I saw my mate Pete, in full uniform and on duty, sitting up at the front of the cart, reins in hands, driving the horse and with two young children sitting in the back of the cart. "What the hell are you doing, Pete?" I enquired.

"No lights, mate. Come on, I'm taking it to the nick."

I walked the short distance with Pete and his newly acquired equine friend to the yard at Limehouse Police Station. Now, although some London police stations do have stables for police horses, Limehouse certainly was not one of them. Pete climbed down and instructed the kids, a boy aged about ten and a girl a couple of years older, to hold the horse while we both went inside to enlighten the duty station sergeant.

"Sarge, I've got a horse and cart in the yard," announced Pete.

"Are you taking the piss, Constable, or what?" enquired the disbelieving sergeant.

"No, Sarge. I found a couple of young kids taking their dad's horse and cart back to its yard on the Island," that's the Isle of Dogs. "He's a totter." A rag and bone and scrap metal dealer. "They haven't got any lights and I thought it best to bring them in as it will soon be lighting-up time."

"Well, you thought wrong, you stupid bastard! It's not yet lighting up time and you could have got them home by now if you hadn't brought them here. What the fuck do you expect me to do with them? Get them out of here! I suggest you walk at the front of the bloody animal waving your torch and your mate walks behind waving his, just get out of here and make bloody sure you get those kids and Dobbin home safely."

Pete and I duly complied with our instructions and found that the kids' dad had left them to get the horse home while he caught a bus. We advised him as to his ill-conceived actions. Pete was convinced he had done the right thing under the circumstances, despite the admonishment from the station sergeant, and on reflection I think he was right. From then on his nickname around the station was Cowboy.

Another day, Pete caused quite a stir and no little annoyance to the duty sergeant at Limehouse when he announced that he had a double-decker bus outside and had arrested all the passengers. He had been patrolling his beat when he was stopped by a bus driver who told him there was a disturbance on the bus. His conductor had been called to the upper deck by a young girl who alleged her purse had been stolen by a group of about twelve youths who were harassing her and causing trouble. Pete climbed the stairs to confront the gang but met with a load of abuse. He told them to return the purse or he would arrest the lot of them, but his threat was met with raucous laughter.

My determined colleague immediately stood at the top of the stairs to prevent any of the suspects from leaving, by which time another patrolling beat officer, who had seen the disturbance, joined Pete on the bus, and instructed the conductor to tell the driver to proceed the short distance to Limehouse nick without stopping, which he did. On describing the incident to the duty sergeant, he was told in no uncertain terms that there were not enough officers on duty to interview the suspects and to "solve the bloody crime himself!" Pete returned to the top deck of the bus and together with the other officer carried out a search and found the girl's missing purse stuffed down the back of a seat.

The girl was delighted, no money was missing and as there was no evidence to indicate who was responsible, none of the suspects were charged. However, Pete did get all their particulars, explained that the bus was not going anywhere until they got off, which they did, at which point the driver then drove off to rejoin his original route.

A practice that was occasionally talked about in police canteens was the game of snooker, not table snooker but "traffic snooker". This was a game specifically played by lads in the traffic division, the dreaded speed cops whose main work consisted of dealing with traffic accidents but who also reported motorists for speeding offences. The game the officers played consisted of scoring points, as in table snooker, the numbers depending on the colours of the cars they had reported for speeding during their shift — for example, a red car scored 1 point, a yellow 2 points, and so on, with a black one scoring the maximum 7 points. At the end of a shift, the traffic cars on the division would return to the police garage and the crews totted up their points to find the winner. I never heard what the prize was.

★ ★ ★

Night Duty on Fridays and Saturdays at Limehouse Police Station was always organized chaos. The local pubs and restaurants were packed with dockers spending their wages, seamen ashore for the night, prostitutes offering their services to willing clients along with the regular numbers of visitors from other parts of London who wanted to enjoy a typical night out in the East End. The result of that cross-section of society mingling together, most fuelled by alcohol, was a very busy tour of duty for the beat bobbies. I loved it. There was never a dull moment, not knowing what incidents would be presented from one minute to the next, while not neglecting the mundane part of everyday policing — road accidents, sudden deaths and old ladies who had locked themselves out of their houses.

If we were called to pub fights they were often over before our arrival. The biggest problem for us at weekends was the number of drunks we had to arrest. Most had been thrown out of pubs or restaurants and were often completely incapable and incoherent. When we arrested a drunk we would attempt to walk them to the police station but if that was impossible we would wait for the patrolling police van to arrive, load them into the back and take them in. On arrival, we would report to the duty station sergeant or inspector, tell them why we had made the arrest (although that was pretty obvious), then wait our turn to process the prisoner. Unlike today, there was little paperwork to complete; notes were made by the arresting officer in his notebook, the prisoner was searched and their property listed and stored, the charge was read by the station sergeant then the arresting officer would sign the charge sheet. Finally the prisoner would be taken to the cells and locked up for the night. The following morning he would be given breakfast and subsequently taken to Thames Magistrates' Court. All fairly straightforward one might think — not quite!

On Friday and Saturday nights the average number of prisoners charged with drunkenness and similar alcohol-related offences at Limehouse was probably about ten or twelve, and on several occasions I counted as many as seventeen or eighteen. Of course, not all prisoners were brought to the station at the same time, but for the couple of hours after pub closing time — which in those days was 10.30 or 11p.m. — things were hectic. Quite often one would see all six beat officers, plus one or two others from the van patrol, in the large charge room with their prisoners at one time. When a prisoner had been processed and locked up, the arresting officer would return to the streets and it was not at all unusual to see a PC return to the nick five minutes later with another prisoner. Two or three arrests for drunkenness by an officer were not uncommon if they were posted to one of the busy beats around East and West India Dock Roads and Commercial Road. I think four arrests in one night was the record. If the cells at Limehouse were full and it was not possible to accommodate all prisoners, some would be taken to Poplar.

Sometimes drunken prisoners would demand to see a doctor, the divisional surgeon, not because they were ill but because they wanted to be examined and told whether or not they were drunk. The station officer would make a decision as to the medical state of a prisoner and call the doctor if he had any doubts, however, drunkenness was not a reason to do so. On several occasions drunks would not take "no" for an answer and would become threatening or perhaps try to smash up a cell, however one of the station sergeants had an unusual way of dealing with such trouble makers.

He would allow a PC to don a white traffic coat, which was sometimes used by the officers on point duty. Seeing the white coat made the drunk think the doctor had arrived, and he (it was usually a man) would be very happy to co-operate with the "doctor", whose "drunkenness test" included asking him to touch his nose, touch his toes and walk in a straight line; of course the inebriated and troublesome prisoner failed the test but was quite content with the result, often thanked the "doctor" for coming to see him, ceased his previous violent behaviour and was happily settled in his cell for the night. Many people would rightly criticize that way of dealing with troublesome and often violent prisoners and it did not happen often; however, it did work and was it not better than two or three officers using physical force to restrain someone, which when witnessed by other drunken prisoners could cause even more problems?

Most drunk prisoners were not too much of a problem except for some vomiting, urinating and worse. Although they might be given a bucket of water and mop when they had sobered up in the morning and told to clean up the cell, some did not do so. I always felt sorry for the station cleaners who had to deal with it.

Many a time I attended family disputes and was met by a distraught female, often with a black eye or similar injury, who had been confronted by her drunken partner on his arrival home from the pub, having spent most of his week's wages, and been hit by him because his dinner was in the bin. Despite her injury, the woman would frequently refuse to make a written allegation or agree to attend court to give evidence against her partner. He would obviously be quite happy with her decision and after receiving my admonition about his behaviour all was considered well.

If an officer made an arrest of any kind he was required to attend court the following morning, on a Monday if made on a weekend. The usual routine was to finish Night Duty at 6a.m., go to bed for two or three hours, have breakfast and then go to court at 10a.m. If the prisoner was charged with a minor offence such as drunk and disorderly, they would invariably plead guilty and, depending on the number of cases to be heard, the officer was free to leave court and return to his bed to get some sleep ready for another Night Duty. Should attendance at court be required when on Night Duty, the officer could claim four hours' overtime regardless of how long he was there. We could attend court up to ten to twelve days during three weeks on Night Duty, therefore we could accrue over forty hours" overtime, which could be taken off in lieu at any time within three months. If taken together with the usual days off it would result in a nice well-earned break.

Being in a dock area, Limehouse had quite a large number of prostitutes and during my time patrolling the beats I got to know some of them fairly well. I invariably felt sorry for them and never had reason to arrest any for offences relating to prostitution, only drunkenness.

Occasionally, a team of officers would be formed, sometimes in plain clothes, specifically to have a purge on the girls for openly soliciting, also premises would be watched and arrests made relating to running brothels. However, the prostitutes I met on the street plied their trade mainly close to the docks and around the public houses where the merchant seamen were to be found.

Of course, some of the girls were funding drug habits and undoubtedly had pimps controlling them, although I saw very little evidence of that. They were more likely to be young single mothers struggling to bring up families, or others who had been thrown out by parents or left home after physical or sexual abuse. I even met one who had been a schoolteacher and, after suffering a nervous breakdown, she told me that she just couldn't face the stress of teaching anymore.

The one thing that surprised me was the honesty of some of the girls. A seaman told me of a particular prostitute he went with on a regular basis when in port and on one trip she found him quite drunk in a pub and openly displaying a large sum of money. He was too drunk to have sex but, fearing for his safety, she took part of the cash off him prior to him going on to another pub. The girl wrote a note telling him what she had done and put it in his pocket, which he found the next day after setting sail. When he returned several weeks later he met her and she readily handed him back his money. Sometimes British seamen might deposit some of their wages with a pub landlord to look after when in port but forget what they had done, however, the cash was handed back when they next returned.

I heard several sad stories from the prostitutes, especially the older ones who looked even older and were often in poor health. Members of the Salvation Army, wearing their easily recognizable uniforms, would regularly visit the Limehouse pubs at weekends to sell their magazine the *War Cry* and chat to the locals. I often saw them chatting to the street girls, presumably offering help. However, I guess the oldest profession in the world has always been the same and the prostitutes' stories that I heard could be repeated the world over.

In addition to touring the Limehouse streets to pick up drunken prisoners, the police van had other uses. One particular Night Duty, we paraded ready for duty and were given some information by the station sergeant that he thought we might be able to assist with. A loveable old lady had come to the station earlier in the evening to report her cat missing. She gave a full description of her precious pet, I think it was named Tiddles, and explained that she would leave a window open at the side of her house so that if a policeman should find her cat during the night he could pop it through. We'd see cats scavenging for food around the bins at the rear of Chinese restaurants and as it was a fairly quiet night the van driver, another experienced copper with a great sense of humour, together with his colleague, decided to tour likely haunts of feline strays. The end result was that during the night they picked up three or four cats took them in the van to the lady's house and posted them through the window! I never heard if the old dear got her Tiddles back, I hope she did, but once again nothing was too much to ask from the friendly bobby on the beat.

In addition to the six beats covered by the Limehouse officers, one constable would patrol the Isle of Dogs, which had a very small police station that was closed to the public at night but to which the PC had access. There was a small walk-tunnel connecting the Isle of Dogs, under the Thames, to Greenwich on the South Bank. The walk took about five minutes and occasionally, when I was posted to the Island and things were quiet in the middle of the night, I would stroll through the tunnel to look at and admire the *Cutty Sark*, an old tea clipper sailing ship built in 1869 which was located immediately opposite the end of the tunnel. I sometimes met a beat officer from Greenwich and we would have a brief chat before I returned to my patch. Such jaunts would undoubtedly have resulted in a severe reprimand for leaving my beat and, more importantly, the division, without good cause, but it didn't occur to me at the time — I suppose I could have made the excuse of following a suspect!

On some occasions cadets who had completed their training at Hendon were posted to police stations for various duties before returning to do their full training prior to being appointed constables. When at a station they gained experience of various aspects of police work, including beat patrols. I recall one such cadet named John Hoddinnot who was posted at Limehouse and who for about a week came out on beat patrol with me.

John was at least six foot six, possibly more, and as we went on to the street together for the first time I jokingly told him that as I was only five foot eight, he should walk behind me so as not to present a chance for the public to laugh at "little and large". He saw the funny side of it, of course. I became quite friendly with John and we played divisional rugby together. After he became a constable and returned to Limehouse he quickly rose through the uniformed ranks, was highly respected and, several years later, as Sir John Hoddinnot, CBE, became Chief Constable of Hampshire. He sadly died suddenly in 2001 at the age of only fifty-six years.

CHAPTER
FOUR

East Enders

When most people hear the phrase "East Enders" they automatically think of the popular television soap opera that has been running for many years. I don't, I think of those wonderful characters I met and worked amongst in and around Limehouse during the 1960s. The television actors are quite good at speaking the language of East End folk but the true character of a born-and-bred cockney is far removed from what we see on the TV.

The one thing that the cockneys project more than anything else is their humour. No matter what situation they find themselves in, they always seem to find some excuse to laugh about it. That was, of course, displayed so vividly when they were on the receiving end of exploding V-2 rockets during the Second World War. If anyone wants to sample cockney humour I suggest that they go to Upton Park, home of West Ham United Football Club, on a Saturday afternoon and listen to the very funny banter and colourful language exchanged between the supporters.

Matches at the ground were policed mainly by officers from East and West Ham Police Stations but when a big game was being played, others were seconded from neighbouring stations. Those match duties were always voluntary and the officers were paid overtime but I never did one. An officer I knew did attend one game though, only one, because he was somehow hit in the face with a kipper thrown by someone in the crowd! I often went to games when off duty and in those days the ground was not all-seating — it was such a funny experience to listen and watch the cockney supporters, most of whom were dock workers, venting their feelings and views on their team — and the referee if they were losing. Bobby Moore, in those early days of his career, was their hero.

Even in the 1960s the East End of London could be called multicultural, with the Jewish, Polish, Chinese and Indian communities already well established and others from some of the Eastern European countries beginning to arrive. The Muslim community did not have the great presence that it does today; the East London Mosque, which can be seen in the Whitechapel Road, was built in 1985. Instead, it was immigrants from the West Indies, Jamaica in particular, who began to settle and black communities started to develop. Many came in the mid to late 1950s as a result of government policy to boost employment in the London Transport system and in the National Health Service. Police training did not include any in-depth training as to the cultures of various nationalities at that time, therefore the beat constable had to quickly learn from experience.

There were a number of black people, particularly men, living in Limehouse and Stepney during my time on the beat and they rarely caused us any problems. They all seemed to work hard, were polite, kept to themselves and I never heard of any real racial problems between them or the local cockney population. The main aim the immigrants had seemed to be to earn enough money to send to their families back home in the Caribbean Islands, and eventually pay for them to come to England. I do remember being called by a very annoyed man who was on shift work but unable to sleep during the day due to the noise coming from next door. On investigating the loud banging I found the occupant, a Jamaican who rented one room, mixing cement and building a brick wall in the centre of the room in order to create two rooms. He explained that he was doing it because his brother was shortly arriving from Jamaica and the room was for him. He added that his landlord, also a Jamaican, had given him permission to do it. I instructed the budding builder to stop his construction and suggested he should ask his landlord about planning permission, which he had never heard of.

There were, of course, one or two well-known crime families familiar to us, but uniformed officers had little to do with them; the last thing they wanted was to draw attention to themselves by being arrested for some minor offence.

The attitude of the public towards crime, criminals and the police was very different to what it is today. The East Enders would often leave their doors unlocked, and on a hot summer evening it was quite usual to see some of the older ones sitting on chairs in the street outside their front doors chatting to each other. The women were so proud of their red-painted front steps and highly polished brass door knockers; a throwback to the war years, I guess. A nice hot cup of "Rosie Lee" was always on offer to the passing beat constable from those lovely people. Working in the East End I had to quickly learn some of the cockney rhyming slang that would be spoken among the market traders and dockers.

In the early 1960s police officers were generally respected by the public, even teenagers. There were exceptions, but we had ways and means of dealing with stroppy youths and the stop and search powers that we had were particularly useful. Some groups of yobs would think it clever to spread across the width of the pavement on the approach of a PC, trying to force him to walk in the road, which we never allowed. A ruse occasionally used by us was to identify the ringleader who was usually the biggest, stop him and ask for his personal details, then ask him where he had been twenty-four hours earlier because he resembled a suspect who had been indecently exposing himself outside the local public toilets. He would account for his whereabouts, which was accepted, but the reaction of his mates was to laugh and ridicule him, which was, of course, our aim. Such police action was obviously not in the training manual but the troublesome yobs had to be taught that they could not get the upper hand as far as the beat officers were concerned.

Cockneys are very proud of their heritage and anyone, especially the younger ones, bringing disgrace on a family could be dealt with fairly harshly, as I once witnessed. I arrested a lad of about fourteen for attempted burglary and, being a juvenile, his parents had to attend the police station in order that he could be bailed to appear at juvenile court. They duly arrived, were informed of the details of their son's arrest and were shown into the charge room, where he was waiting. On seeing his miscreant son, the father rushed at him and started to give him what can only be described as a good hiding.

"How many times have I told you that if you carry on like this you'll end up in prison like me!" he yelled.

I had to pull the man off the boy as I feared if he carried on I would have to arrest him for assault. The lad had been left in no doubt that he had let his family down.

Now it seems that some will use any excuse to complain about police behaviour but that didn't seem to happen so much in the early 1960s. One incident happened to a colleague of mine at another station on the division. A man had been arrested for attempting to indecently assault a nine-year-old boy in the toilets at the Tower of London. The lad had gone into the Gents while his parents waited outside and when he came out he told them that a man had taken him into a cubicle and tried to assault him but he had escaped. The boy pointed out the disappearing assailant to a police officer who made the arrest, and all parties were taken to the station. The offender was placed in a cell while the boy's father sat on a bench in the charge room, which was adjacent to the divisional surgeon's room where the boy had gone with his mother awaiting a medical examination.

Word had got round the station that a male had been arrested at the Tower of London for indecently assaulting a young boy. One of the older constables walked into the charge room and on seeing a man sitting on the bench, assumed that he was the alleged offender.

"You dirty bastard!" he yelled and hit the man across the head knocking him to the floor.

The duty inspector, on hearing the commotion, quickly entered the room, picked the man off the floor and informed the officer that he had hit the boy's father not the prisoner ... What could have been an extremely serious situation, which would undoubtedly have ended the experienced officer's career, was defused and resolved by the surprising reaction of the father. He stated that he wanted no action taken, didn't want to make a complaint and fully understood the officer's reaction, adding, "I only hope that you give that treatment to the bastard who interfered with my son."

That, of course, did not happen but the offender was subsequently jailed.

I was proud of the fact that during my police service I never had a complaint made by a member of the public against me. Some officers used to believe that if nobody complained about you then you can't have been carrying out your job but I never subscribed to that. One person who did have a complaint made against him was a friend of mine — a true Londoner and a real comedian, although perhaps his cockney sense of humour wasn't always appreciated.

My friend had finished his time patrolling beats and transferred to the traffic patrol unit. In those days, officers used to ride either low-powered motorcycles nicknamed "Noddy Bikes" or more powerful motorbikes. One particular day, he was riding a Noddy Bike and stopped at a red traffic light. A man riding a motorbike and sidecar pulled up alongside and my friend noticed that the man had his small dog in the sidecar. "I see you are taking your wife out for an airing," quipped my friend. That comment resulted in the one and only complaint against him in thirty years' service, for which he received a written caution.

Although it may sound unbelievable, it wasn't uncommon for a cockney offender to say when being arrested, "OK, it's a fair cop, Guv." I often felt a little embarrassed having to repeat the phrase when giving evidence at court, and I wondered if the magistrate thought I was "verbaling" the accused. The "verbal" was something that an East End offender, and others, often referred to and hated. Their definition of the word was "Something that a police officer would falsely allege the prisoner had said when questioned or arrested", despite the fact that their rights were protected by the Official Police Caution that they need not say anything. The astute officer, when cross-examined in court and asked by a defending barrister what a "verbal" was, would reply that it was a true statement made by a defendant that was alleged by a defence barrister to be false when he had a weak case. Experienced lawyers never asked the question.

Later, as a detective, I and another officer arrested a man in South London for murder, a stabbing. When we put him in a police car and told him he was being arrested for murder we searched him and found a large number of amphetamine tablets in his pocket. On taking them from him he said, "You can't take those off me, they're my licence to kill." That statement was strongly challenged by his barrister at the subsequent Old Bailey trial and I think some, including a few police officers, thought it was a "verbal" I had made up and accredited to him — it certainly wasn't, it was absolutely true.

Christmas was a particularly great time to be on duty patrolling the streets of Limehouse. Over the holiday period it was customary for single officers to work and enable the married ones to take time off. I worked over the Christmas holidays in 1962 and 1963 and was lucky enough to be on Late Turn during the former and Night Duty for the latter. I was invited into numerous homes for a sherry and a mince pie by residents who had seen me patrolling the streets. I lost count of the number of Boxing Day parties I was invited to and, believe me, the East Enders knew how to party — they were one big knees-up and sing-along! The aim of some female revellers was to kiss the copper under the mistletoe and I was not allowed to leave the festivities until I had obliged. It was difficult to get away but the beat still had to be patrolled — until the next party.

All the officers on beat duty had similar experiences, the effects of which were fairly apparent when they returned to the station. It was also quite common for several of the local folk to call at the police station with a tray of mince pies, sausage rolls or turkey sandwiches over the Christmas period. One Chinese restaurant would also bring in food. I guess today officially none of that would be allowed, the gifts would be classed as gratuities. The thoughtfulness and kindness of those wonderful folk would be rejected, but I am convinced that if given and taken in the right spirit, which I witnessed, then the relationship between the police and the public could only be enhanced. After all, when did you last see a police officer patrolling his beat on Christmas Day?

I also have fond memories not just of Limehouse, but of the East End of London generally. My colleagues and I, and later my family, often took advantage of what it had to offer — the pie and mash shops with the wonderful liquor that they served with it; the bakery in Bethnal Green that sold freshly baked smoked salmon and onion bagels in the middle of the night. Then there was Tubby Isaac's jellied eel and shellfish stall in Aldgate, which opened at about 8p.m. and remained open until about 2a.m. It was literally world famous and I lost count of the numbers of people from all walks of life who I saw there enjoying their bowls of jellied eels, cockles, mussels and whelks. Many party and theatregoers would stop at Tubby's stall on their way home to the East End after a night out Up West. I was recently delighted to hear that, although Tubby Isaacs died several years ago, his stall is still in business.

Another world famous establishment in Whitechapel was Blooms Restaurant in Brick Lane, which specialized in Jewish kosher food. Diners came from all over London to sample it, and I can still taste and smell the fantastic salt beef sandwiches that we would get after a Late Turn.

I thoroughly recommend that anyone wishing to visit the East End should go to Petticoat Lane on a Sunday morning; it is located in Middlesex Street, near Aldgate East station. Visitors from all over the world go there to have a look round this very old and historic London street market. The numerous stalls sell just about everything one would expect, but it is not just the goods sold that are the attractions, it is the stallholders. The tradition of working there has been passed down through generations in some families, and the true cockney humour can be seen and witnessed on many stalls. However, if visiting, beware: Petticoat Lane has everything — pickpockets, card tricksters and conmen — and, as with any street market, not all the goods sold are genuine brands, some are fake copies.

Three particular public houses I frequented with my friends when off duty were the Watermans Arms and Pride of the Isle, both on the Isle of Dogs on the Limehouse patch, and the Prospect of Whitby at Wapping. The landlord of the Watermans Arms was

Daniel Farson, a well-known television personality at the time, and most evenings it was quite usual to see show-business friends of Daniel's at the pub enjoying the music and entertainment. The Pride of the Isle was a very popular pub that had great entertainment every night, featuring drag artists — in that era, with the exception of the East End pubs, pantomime dames and Danny La Rue's club in Soho, effeminate men dressed up as women were a novelty. Some of the performers at the Pride were absolutely hilarious.

The Prospect of Whitby was and still is a very well-known pub on the north bank of the Thames and, particularly during the long summer evenings, it would be packed with customers enjoying the river views. The original pub dates back to 1543 when it was known as the Devil's Tavern. It burned down and was rebuilt, and by the seventeenth century it was frequented by smugglers and villains and, prior to his arrest, by the infamous "Hanging" Judge Jeffreys, who would sit by the river supping ale and watching the public hangings at the nearby "hanging dock".

Another famous pub that can still be visited today is the Town of Ramsgate, originally called The Hostel and then, in 1533, The Red Cow, in Anchor and Hope Alley, just off Wapping High Street. It dates back to the Wars of the Roses in the 1460s and is one of the oldest pubs on the river. It was there that "Hanging" Judge Jeffreys was captured in 1688 while trying to flee the country and was sent to the nearby Tower of London where he died. It is interesting to learn that in those days there were about thirty-six ale houses, mostly of ill repute, in Wapping High Street alone and approximately 140 in the area.

A pub I have good reason to be nostalgic about was in Bethnal Green, although I can't recall the name. It was a very lively establishment and not only promoted professional acts each night, including singers, comedians and drag artists, but encouraged customers to go onto the stage and perform. Those brave enough to do so had to be good. A great act was a chap who dressed as a cowboy, entered the bar via a side door on a beautiful white horse and sang country-and-western songs. One evening, a colleague and I took my future wife and two of her nursing friends to the pub — the three girls were known for their singing abilities at the West London Hospital where they worked and were probably, I thought, good enough to become a professional singing trio. On hearing the pub compère asking for customers to perform, after much persuasion the girls went up and sang two songs, for which they received great applause from the clientele. In fact, they paid for our drinks for the rest of the night! The compère told the girls that they would be welcome to sing any time they visited the pub, however, they decided to retire at the top and did not go back.

There are numerous stories told of East End crimes and of course the best known is the Jack the Ripper murders when, between 1888 and 1891, up to eleven women, most of whom were prostitutes, were brutally mutilated and murdered by a serial killer in the Whitechapel area. The crimes were investigated by detectives from Leman Street police station, but were never solved. Other notorious crimes include the shooting dead of criminal George Cornell by Ronnie Kray, one of the infamous twins, in March 1966, as he sat on a stool in the bar of the Blind Beggar in the Whitechapel Road. Opposite that pub can be found the Royal London Hospital where the remains of poor John Merrick, made famous in the film *The Elephant Man*, are still kept. Cable Street was where a constable was murdered many years ago and his body put down a drain. Another part of history took place with the Siege of Sidney Street, Stepney in 1911 when 200 police officers battled with criminals hiding in No 100 for over six hours. Winston Churchill, then Home Secretary, came to take charge. He refused to allow the fire brigade to enter, and the standoff eventually ended after the building was consumed with fire.

A tragic event took place during the Second World War at Bethnal Green Underground Station on 3 March 1943. During the war years many London tube stations were used as air raid shelters. When the siren sounded warning of an imminent air raid, members of the public would be directed by police officers and wardens down into the stations, where they remained until the raid was over — sometimes all night. Bethnal Green was one of the stations used for such a purpose. On that tragic night 173 people including sixty children were suffocated and crushed to death and many more were injured when panic to get to the safety of the underground developed into a stampede. An air raid siren had indicated a possible attack, but at the same time the sound of anti-aircraft guns that were being fired from nearby Victoria Park was mistaken for enemy aircraft fire and people entering the station panicked. Unfortunately it had been raining, the steps down to the underground were wet and slippery and there were no hand rails, causing those people at the front to fall and those behind to pile up on top of them.

When working as a police officer in all those areas I was very much aware of the history attached to them and I felt privileged to have walked their streets. I often think how different my experiences might have been if I had patrolled the beat in one of the more rural, leafy suburbs of London. I'm sure officers who did could tell many fascinating stories and it would be interesting to compare our diverse experiences, but for me the East End was best.

I have thought about returning to my old haunts in the East End of London and I wonder what the present cockneys who still live there make of it all today. I know everything has changed: the buildings, the roads, the people and the whole environment. Indeed, I suppose I wouldn't recognize some of the places now, and that's what probably holds me back from making a pilgrimage.

Perhaps the nature of the true cockneys that I knew can best be portrayed by one who would always stop for a chat with the beat bobby when on his way at lunchtimes to his local pub. He had drunk there for over sixty years. Charlie was a widower and died at the age of eighty-five, but prior to doing so he arranged his own funeral and left strict instructions as to how it should be conducted. Subsequently, the funeral cortege stopped outside the old boy's favourite watering hole on the way to the crematorium; all his drinking mates came out, surrounded the hearse and drank a toast to their departed pal with pints of Guinness, his favourite daily tipple. The old boy had, over a period of time before his death, deposited money with the publican to pay not only for those drinks and many more but also for jellied eels, cockles, mussels and whelks from Tubby Isaac's shellfish stall in Aldgate, which everyone could enjoy when they returned from the crematorium.

When I finished duty that day I and two other beat bobbies went to the pub where a real old cockney knees-up and sing-song was taking place and we were pleased to enjoy a bowl of eels and drink our toast to Charlie, a much-loved true cockney.

CHAPTER
FIVE

Incidents and Arrests

Most police officers who have served at busy London police stations have numerous stories to tell — exciting, frightening, sad and funny and some stories that, although true, are quite unbelievable. My tales are no exception. As the saying goes, real life is stranger than fiction.

I will always remember my first arrest. I had finished my three weeks of patrolling with another officer and was out on patrol alone on Night Duty for the first time. I noticed a middle-aged woman, obviously very drunk, staggering towards me on East India Dock Road, shouting and swearing. I told her that I was arresting her for being drunk and disorderly and took hold of her arm, whereupon she kneed me in the groin — not hard, but enough to make my eyes water. I managed to get her to the station and gave the facts to the station officer, including the knee to the groin.

He laughed. "Oh, she always does that to a new copper she doesn't know when she gets pissed."

Evidently this poor woman was an alcoholic prostitute named Betty, aged about thirty-five and looking sixty-five, who had numerous convictions for being drunk and soliciting and was well known to the lads on the beat. I felt sorry for her and because the knee to my groin had caused me no more than a minor temporary discomfort, I decided not to press for a charge of Assault on Police. The next day, Betty appeared at the magistrates' court, pleaded guilty to being drunk and was given a very small fine. She did not remember her assault on my wedding tackle but when informed of it apologized, telling me to tell my girlfriend that she was sorry!

I remember exactly where I was at midnight on 31 December 1962. Wrestling on the ground in about a foot of snow with a drunken man I had just arrested. Near Limehouse Police Station was a Salvation Army hostel for men, which looked after the needs of the homeless, alcoholics and the usual lost souls, of which there were many at that time in London's East End. Those staying at the hostel would pay for one night's lodging or longer, and if lucky enough their bill was paid for by social services. We were very frequently called to the premises to eject an occupant who was causing trouble or to arrest some drunk. A complaint I often heard from the occupants was that they had paid for a week's lodging and after the first night they had been ejected and barred because their bed had been found wet by the staff. The complaint was either against some unknown resident who did not like the complainant or against the staff who wanted the bed in order to make more money from a new resident. I found that rather worrying as it seemed refunds were never given to those ejected. They were just put back out on the streets.

On that New Year's Eve it had been snowing heavily. I was called to the hostel and asked to eject a man who was drunk and who had stayed the previous night and wet his bed. I took his arm to support him and told him I was arresting him. As we walked through the hostel grounds the local clock struck midnight, fireworks lit the sky, and the ships in the West India Docks, of which there were many in those days, sounded their sirens. The drunk, who I was supporting, said to me in a very slurred voice, "No hard feelings, Copper, let me shake your hand and wish you a Happy New Year."

"Certainly. Happy New Year," I said, offering him my right hand while still supporting him under his right shoulder with my left arm. Instead of shaking my hand the ungrateful sod pushed hard with his shoulder into my chest, the result being that we both ended up on the frozen ground rolling around in about a foot of snow. I was trying to regain my professional dignity and get to my feet and he was attempting to get up and run, but finding the effects of the alcohol he had consumed made it doubly difficult. I helped him up and there we were, both covered in soft snow. At that moment a colleague appeared in case I needed any assistance. Seeing the state of the pair of snowmen he burst out laughing, made a snowball, threw it at me and enquired, "What the hell are you doing? You were sent to nick the bugger not challenge him to a snowball fight!"

We made it back to the police station where everyone was wishing each other a Happy New Year. I didn't mention my little fracas, the drunk appeared at court the following day, received a conditional discharge and was wished a Happy New Year by the magistrate.

That same winter, which was particularly severe, I arrested another poor man whom I have always remembered because he was blind. I found him wandering around tapping his white stick at about 11 o'clock at night, fairly close to the Salvation Army hostel. He told me that he had been turned away as there were no beds available and he also had no money or lodging vouchers. He was absolutely frozen and asked me if I could take him to the station and give him a bed for the night. I explained that was not possible, I could only take him in if I arrested him. He agreed quite readily to be arrested and charged with being drunk in a public place, although it was very evident that he had not been drinking. I took him to the station where he was duly charged, given a cup of hot tea and a sandwich, a warm cell with a mattress and blanket, all of which he could not thank me enough for.

The next morning, after a good police breakfast, the blind man appeared at Thames Magistrates' Court. One or two comments were made by other officers describing me as "a bit of a bastard" for nicking a blind man. I ignored them. The man pleaded guilty to the charge of being drunk and was given a very small fine or seven days in prison. I asked him if I could pay his fine, and gave him a few shillings with which to get a bus to a social welfare office — he was delighted. I never saw the blind man on our patch again.

Asking to be arrested was not unusual in the cold weather, especially in the week prior to Christmas. One poor old boy named Alfie was well known to all the officers at Limehouse, to whom he was always polite and called them "Sir". He lived rough on the streets and rarely spoke to anyone. He seemed to have very little money, claimed no benefits and existed on food being given to him by local restaurants and shops. Alfie was very intelligent and had apparently once been an academic lecturer, his subject being history. His wife had died in middle age, he had no children or relatives and just couldn't cope with life. He had a breakdown and took to living on the streets. When the weather was cold, Alfie would ask to be arrested for begging and would be charged under the Vagrancy Act 1824, knowing that he would get seven days in prison, where he would be warm, fed, washed and provided with a new set of clothes ready to continue with his tough street existence. At Christmas, he would always ask to be arrested in order to get a Christmas dinner. Were we, as police officers, helping the likes of Alfie to abuse the system? Perhaps, but I believe that giving a small helping hand to someone living an abject existence pales into insignificance when one sees the abuse of social services that goes on today.

Another cheeky chappie I arrested had his request granted to be sent back to prison where he was most happy. He approached me in Commercial Road and told me he had come out of prison only that morning after serving six months, adding that he couldn't cope with the cold weather that day and wanted to go back inside. I told him that if he got drunk he might well be arrested, but no, that wasn't good enough for him. For being drunk he knew he would only get a fine or at the most seven days' imprisonment. He wanted much longer!

"If I chuck a brick through a shop window, that would do it, wouldn't it?" he cheekily enquired.

"I suppose it would but I wouldn't suggest you do it," I advised.

The next thing I saw was him crossing the busy road and about to carry out his threat. Without me seeing, he picked up a brick from a nearby building site and hurled it through Boots the chemist's shop window. I strolled over, cautioned him and made one of the easiest arrests ever — if only they were all like that. The next morning, the joker appeared at court and pleaded guilty. After hearing my evidence of the offence, and the conversation which preceded it, and taking into account his previous convictions, the magistrate said he was happy to "act as fairy Godfather and grant you your wish", and sentenced him to six months. Another satisfied customer.

A task that a police officer does not like but has to do is informing relatives or friends that a loved one has died or been involved in an accident. One afternoon, it was my duty to go to a rundown block of flats on my beat to deliver a message that had come through on the station teleprinter from Newcastle Police. I knocked on the door and was shortly confronted by a very large, elderly cockney woman, her hair in curlers and covered with the obligatory head scarf.

"Mrs Griffin?" I enquired.

"Yes, oh Christ, what now?"

"I am sorry to inform you that your husband has died up in Newcastle."

Crying, tears tantrums? No, just the reply "Good! Thank Christ, at last. I have hated that old bastard for years! Would you like a cup of tea, young man?" I politely declined the offer and continued on my beat patrol.

Early one morning I knocked on a door to inform a lady that her husband had been knocked off his bicycle while on his way to work. Two people came to the door, the wife and daughter. I explained what had happened and that although the husband had been taken to Poplar Hospital he was not badly injured. Being helpful I continued, "in fact if you phone the Accident and Emergency department at the hospital you might well be able to have a word with him." With that the lady fainted, falling forward into my arms. The daughter then started crying. "My dad's deaf and dumb!"

We managed to get the lady indoors, where she recovered and, after a strong cup of tea, I returned to my beat.

Death is always a difficult subject to deal with in whatever shape or form, perhaps especially if it has come about due to a road accident. It was about 1 a.m. on a dark, wet night and I was patrolling a beat on the Isle of Dogs. The main road round that area was

Westferry Road, horseshoe shaped with sharp bends and high brick walls on either side, separating it from the West India Docks. I had just walked round one of the bends when behind me I heard the screech of brakes followed by a deafening crash. I ran the few yards back round the bend and saw a sight I will never forget. Embedded in the wall was a small white van that had been reduced to less than half its original size by the impact. I was able to force open the back doors and the sight was horrific. There were four occupants in the vehicle, all appeared young, two men in the front and two women lying on top of them obviously having been thrown forward from the back. The only sound was the hissing of water from a broken radiator and one of the girls moaning.

I managed to climb into the back of the van and reach forward to her. She was not trapped and I helped her to crawl backwards out of the wreckage. She seemed semi-conscious and her face looked dreadfully injured. I realized that the other three occupants were all trapped and I could do nothing to free them. By then, two other motorists had stopped and I instructed one to drive to the nearest phone box and request that all three of the emergency services attend, including two ambulances. I took off my greatcoat and placed it over the injured girl, who was by this time lying on the pavement. Help arrived within a few minutes. The firemen cut the roof off the van and after some difficulty extracted the three casualties from the wreckage. All four were taken to Poplar Hospital, where the three who had been trapped were tragically pronounced dead. The girl who survived suffered horrific injuries, especially to the face, and was operated on through the night.

I left the scene for the traffic police to deal with and returned to the station. It was the first fatal accident I had dealt with, and although all the training at Peel House had prepared me well for handling and taking control of such an incident, nothing could have prepared me for the feeling of complete numbness that I experienced as I sat in the canteen writing up the accident report. However, my feelings were soon to be tested to the limit.

After completing the report, the duty inspector instructed me to go to the hospital. I was to meet the relatives of the victims and take them to the hospital mortuary so they could formally identify the bodies to me. On arrival, there were mothers, fathers, brothers and sisters who had already been informed of the death of their loved ones. The three sets of parents then identified their children, which was required for a future coroner's inquest. It was noticeable that all three bodies seemed relatively unmarked compared to their friend who had so far survived, and the subsequent post-mortems showed that all three had died from severe internal injuries. The seat belt law had not come into force at that time. Words are superfluous under such circumstances; I said very little to the relatives and left them to grieve in their own way.

Several weeks later, I attended Poplar Coroners' Court, where I gave my evidence relating to the accident. I learned that all four people involved were in their late teens. One of the boys had taken the van, which belonged to his brother, without his permission, not having a licence or insurance, and spent the evening drinking in a local pub. They were on their way home when the driver lost control of the car on the Isle of Dogs" bends. The coroner's verdict was recorded as Accidental Death. What a tragic waste of young lives.

Outside the court I spoke to the only survivor, the young girl I had helped out of the wreckage. She remembered nothing of the crash. She was a lovely looking eighteen-year-old girl but her face had been terribly scarred and disfigured. Her attitude was remarkable, however. Although she had lost her best friend and boyfriend in the crash, had had three big facial operations and faced further skin grafts and bone reconstruction, she told me she was continuing her college studies and looking forward to the future, hopefully becoming a nurse. I sincerely hope she succeeded.

Another fatal accident that I dealt with occurred one night when I was on duty at Poplar. The beat I was patrolling covered the Blackwall Tunnel under the River Thames. It was always busy and Poplar Police Station was responsible for half the length and dealt with any incident that occurred there. It was raining heavily and the road in the tunnel was wet and quite slippery. A young lad was taking his girlfriend home on the back of his motorbike and as he negotiated a slight bend the back wheel slid from under him. He managed to stay on as the bike went over but his girlfriend on the pillion fell off in the path of a large lorry that was travelling in

86

the opposite direction. Her head went under one of the wheels and was completely crushed. Her boyfriend was uninjured but hysterical and I gently led him away from the scene to allow the traffic police to deal with the incident. I never saw him again after that but I often wondered what effect the events of that night had on the poor lad's life.

Of course, we didn't just find problems on the street — they also came to us.

One morning I was handing in an accident report and discussing it with the station sergeant. An elderly man came to the counter and said, "I have just killed my wife."

The ever-unflappable sergeant replied, "Yes, OK, have a seat. I will be with you in a minute."

When he was ready, the sergeant addressed the man. "Now, you have killed your wife, have you? How? Where is she?"

"I strangled her. She's in the wardrobe."

My senior officer had had previous dealings with the man and suspected that he was somewhat mentally unstable, as he had made the same false allegation in the past. He instructed me to take him back to his house and check the wardrobe. I did so and was totally unprepared for what happened next. As I opened the wardrobe door, the lifeless body of the man's wife fell out at my feet. She had a tie around her neck and was well past the possibility of resuscitation. I cautioned the husband and told him that I was arresting him on suspicion of murder. I phoned the station and shortly after the CID arrived and took over. The man later appeared at the Old Bailey, pleaded guilty to manslaughter on the ground of diminished responsibility and was sent to a secure mental institution.

On another occasion I was assisting in the front office, dealing with members of the public who came in with all sorts of problems. We were rarely surprised with what they presented to us, which could be anything from simply asking directions, domestic disputes, noisy neighbours and, of course, the little old lady who often came in with a bag of apples for the lads. On this particular day there were about four or five customers waiting to present their problems. A middle-aged man with a plastic carrier bag entered and went straight to the front of the queue. "I've just robbed a bank and want to give myself up," he announced.

"Yes, but wait in the queue, will you? These people were here before you," instructed the sergeant, whereupon the man duly obliged.

About a minute later, the reserve officer came from the telephone communications room at the back of the front office and informed us that a robbery had just taken place at a bank down the road. The sergeant immediately went to the back of the queue of waiting public and took the arm of the man with the carrier bag, "I think you'd better jump the queue, Sunshine, don't you?"

They went to the charge room, where the bag was tipped out and hundreds of pounds of bank notes fell out on the table. It transpired that the bank robber was another person who had very recently been released from a long prison sentence and wanted to go back inside to be looked after at the taxpayers' expense. He had walked into the bank, threatened the cashier, saying he had a gun (although he had no weapon), stuffed the notes in his bag, and quite casually, strolled the short distance to the police station. In those days, the banks didn't have the sophisticated security systems that they have today. He later appeared at the Inner London Sessions, now called Crown Court, pleaded guilty and was sent to prison for five years.

One quiet Sunday, mid-morning, a sad middle-aged individual presented herself at the station front desk, crying. She said that it was her birthday, she had received no cards from her children, that her husband had recently left her, that she did not wish to carry on living and was going to cut her throat to end it all. The station sergeant knew that there was no woman officer on duty but one of the older very experienced and respected PCs, a real life "Dixon of Dock Green", was in the canteen enjoying a cup of tea. The sobbing woman was told to take a seat at the front desk while he fetched the constable. One can imagine the shock when the two officers returned to find the woman kneeling on the floor with a knife in her hand and in the process of attempting to cut her throat. The PC leaped over the front counter and grabbed the knife. Luckily, she had only suffered superficial cuts. The poor soul was taken to hospital and admitted. I don't know what happened to her but I wonder if her children ever realized what difference sending their mum a couple of birthday cards might have made?

★　★　★

It is amazing how what at first seems harsh action taken by a police officer can in fact later be seen as an act of kindness. I remember being called to a small general store in Limehouse where the owner had caught a lady of about eighty years old stealing a tomato. The shopkeeper said she had frequently stolen items of food from the shop, and although she had been regularly warned she continued with her attempts to steal. The shopkeeper was at his wit's end and as a last resort insisted on charging the old lady with the theft of one tomato, which legally he was entitled to do. I was not happy about his decision but he was very adamant and signed the charge sheet. She appeared at Thames Magistrates' Court about a week later and once again one or two remarks were made about me arresting an old lady just to keep my arrest figures up; totally untrue, no pressure was ever put on us to make arrests.

The old soul admitted the offence and the critics I think changed their opinion when I gave the magistrate the facts. I had found that the old lady lived in squalor, was too proud to have claimed benefits of any sort. Her daughter, who was an invalid, lived in another part of the country and had no idea her mother was in such dire straits. No help had ever been asked for from her neighbours. The lady was simply living a dreadful existence and only stole food because she was starving.

In the interim period between her arrest and appearance at court I requested a social worker attend the hearing and, as a result, the court was told that social services had taken over the case. The old lady's flat had been cleaned up, she had been supplied with food, her gas had been reconnected and she had been persuaded to accept the benefits that were due to her.

The magistrate gave the stubborn old girl an Absolute Discharge and commented that the shopkeeper should not be criticized for his actions because if it was not for him the lady's poor circumstances may not have come to light. The shopkeeper later told me that after the case he sent a box of food round to her. Throughout my career I arrested many people for very serious offences, including murder, but I can honestly say arresting the old lady for stealing a tomato was one that I am quite proud of.

Another shoplifter I dealt with was strange but not that unusual. She was a middle-aged woman who was reasonably well off and had a husband and two teenage children. She was arrested for stealing perfume from Boots and the manager was happy to proceed with a charge of theft. It was always the practice of the police to search the home of a prisoner before they were bailed to appear at court. The woman had told me that she had other stolen goods at home but I was surprised when I took her to her house and discovered an Aladdin's cave. A bedroom at the top of the house, which was not used by the family and evidently always kept locked, was piled from floor to ceiling with stolen goods — everything imaginable — household goods, clothing, toiletries, electrical goods, even pet food, although they had no pets. All the items were still in the original packaging and unopened. She had stolen nothing for her own use and had no intention of selling anything.

The strange thing was that the woman's husband and children said they knew nothing of what she had been up to — and I believed them. They simply had no need to go into the spare bedroom, hadn't done so for several months, and they were genuinely shocked. The lady had no excuse for her actions other than that she was going through the menopause, was bored with life and stealing gave her a thrill. All the stolen property was returned to the rightful owners and she was placed on probation for two years.

Another hoarder I arrested was what one would describe as a "cat burglar". He only committed his crimes in the middle of the night and gained entry to premises by climbing drainpipes. I encountered him at about 3a.m., walking down a backstreet in Stepney, carrying a fairly large bag. In the 1960s the stop and search law was one of the best pieces of legislation that we could use to prevent crime. It meant we could stop and search anyone who we suspected of committing a crime. A man carrying such a bag at that time of the night, and crossing the road on seeing me, certainly fitted the description of a suspected person. I thought it unlikely he was on his way to work and decided to stop him.

We've all seen cartoons depicting Burglar Bill, with his striped shirt, mask and gloves, and carrying a bag marked "swag". The character I stopped that night fitted that description in nearly every respect.

"Excuse me, Sir, where are you going at this time of night?" I enquired.

"I'm just off home, Officer," he replied in a very well spoken, upper-class accent.

"And where have you come from?"

"A house up the road," and that turned out to be true in more ways than one.

"What have you got in your bag?" He said nothing and opened it.

I was astonished to see, apart from a mask, gloves, shoe covers made from two carrier bags and a torch, a silver cruet set and an expensive-looking pen-and-pencil set in a presentation box. The man admitted having burgled a house just a short distance away and I arrested him for the offence.

When the night CID officer and I later searched his house we found in a cupboard in his bedroom a large number of items that had been stolen from various houses in several parts of east London. The loot comprised of mainly silver items, ornaments, clocks and several small paintings that were of little value.

The burglar was very polite and cooperative but his story was rather strange. He was about forty years old, unmarried, lived with his elderly mother and was a civil servant working in a department of the Home Office in Whitehall. He gave the impression of being very much a loner and this was confirmed later by people he worked with. He made a statement, in which he gave the reason for his nocturnal activities as being depressed with his daily life of a boring job and looking after his elderly, senile mother. His criminal activities gave him a thrill and although he had gained entry to premises mainly by climbing drainpipes and through open windows, he had never disturbed or confronted any victims of his burglaries — this was true. He never sold any of the stolen property, which was ultimately returned to the owners.

The man later appeared at court, pleaded guilty to burglary, asked for eight other similar offences to be taken into consideration and was sentenced to two years in prison. He of course lost his employment at the Home Office.

I am sure that nothing in life would shock or surprise me after experiencing some of the strangest incidents that confronted me during my time on the beat. Although every police officer who served in areas such as East London could relate stories similar to those that I have described, I doubt there are many who could claim anything like my next story, which I emphasize is absolutely true.

It is probably not remarkable that most of the interesting incidents I encountered happened on Late Turn or Night Duty, and this was no exception, occurring at about 1 a.m. It was raining heavily when I was called to a small semi-detached house in Poplar where the occupant had been awoken by a dreadful noise coming from his next-door neighbour's garden. The neighbour, who it transpired was rather strange, lived alone and kept half a dozen chickens in the garden. He had been to his local pub for the evening, come home, gone into his garden and attempted to have sexual intercourse with his favourite chicken. The latter had, naturally, objected and with feathers flying made a hell of a noise, which had woken up the neighbour.

I went to the culprit's house, where I found him very drunk, covered in mud and looking quite dishevelled. I couldn't get much sense out of him but arrested him and phoned for the police van to pick us up. I did not take the chicken into custody, although one of my colleagues later suggested I should have taken them all in so that the neighbour could pick out the poor victim on an identification parade.

The next day the man appeared at the magistrates' court charged with committing an act of bestiality. He remembered little of the night before, was obviously very embarrassed, pleaded guilty and was given a twelve months conditional discharge. I think the story appearing in the local paper was enough punishment. Needless to say, for several days there were many jokes circulating around the station about me and the man who became known as "the fowl fucker", and I lost count of the times I was asked how I intended to stuff the family turkey that year!

A very unusual and rare offence came to light late one evening when I was on patrol in the police van with two other officers. We received a radio message from the station to go to a suspected break-in at the local mortuary. It was in a particularly cold winter spell and, as was usual under those conditions, an above-average number of old folk had died — this was long before the winter fuel allowance was brought in.

We found a window broken at the back of the building and on entering we found a youth, aged about fifteen, hiding in a back room. We detained him, searched him and found a knife with a blade about four inches long in his pocket. On going into the post-mortem room we saw a number of bodies that had been pulled out from the freezers. A couple had obviously had post-mortems carried out on them but one other had not, and showed signs of possible knife cuts and stabbing. We arrested the youth and called for the CID to attend and take over the investigation, which subsequently showed that the boy had stabbed one dead body. The offence caused a considerable amount of head scratching among the senior officers as to what the charge should be, he obviously could not be charged with murder, and after consulting the police solicitors the boy was charged with interfering with the work of a coroner.

A few days prior to this, several small deer that were kept in a children's zoo in a park in Hackney, not far from the mortuary, had been killed and others badly mutilated. The youth we had arrested admitted that offence for which he was also charged.

After being remanded in custody and undergoing psychiatric reports the boy was eventually sent to Borstal, which was the equivalent of today's young offenders' institutions but with a much harsher regime. What must go through a young lad's mind to commit such heinous crimes?

★   ★   ★

I dealt with one case of suicide while I was in uniform at Limehouse which was as the result of being called while patrolling my beat by a neighbour of the deceased.

The old man had not been seen for a couple of days and his milk was still on his doorstep. I broke a window with my truncheon, climbed in and found the poor fellow in his bathroom hanging from a pipe above the bath. He had a thick piece of cord round his neck and was visibly dead. His neighbour told me that the old man's wife had died a few weeks before. Although such incidents can affect one and it took a few days for me to get the sight of the hanging man out of my mind, I quickly learned from more experienced officers that a good copper can have feelings for villains and victims but it is vital to just get on with the job in a professional manner.

I investigated two suicide cases later when in the CID and one I particularly remember was an old lady, a widow living alone, who took an overdose of drugs, cut her wrists and lay down to die in her garden at the back of a shed. It was sad, but there was nothing too unusual about the circumstances. A detective colleague, on meeting the lady's son at the house and being told that the place would have to be sold, made an offer and subsequently purchased the property. He did not divulge the history of the house to his wife — I don't think she ever found out.

I also dealt with an alleged rape case. At about midnight while on beat patrol a girl came running up to me crying and told me she had been raped. She was sixteen years old and said she had been grabbed from behind by a complete stranger, who she would not be able to recognize as it was dark, dragged at knifepoint into a nearby allotment and sexually attacked. I went to a nearby police phone box and asked for the van to pick us up. I also requested that any available police cars go to the area where the alleged attack had taken place and stop any suspicious male, although the girl could not give a description.

On arriving at the police station the girl calmed down fairly quickly and a very experienced WPC was instructed to look after her. In those days there weren't special suites for victims of sexual attacks but they were always treated very sympathetically and experienced women police and CID officers would carry out the investigation.

This enquiry suddenly took a dramatic turn. The WPC informed the girl that she would be examined by a doctor, the police divisional surgeon. Every police division had several GPs appointed who would be called to a station at any time to examine victims of crime or prisoners who may have injuries or were sick. When the girl was told this she immediately admitted that she had made up the whole story. She had been at her boyfriend's house all evening and was supposed to be home by 11 o'clock. Knowing that she would be in a lot of trouble, especially from her father who was very strict, she decided to make up the rape allegation.

The parents were phoned shortly after their daughter's admission and told that she was at the police station after being found walking home and was there for her safety; they were not told of the rape allegation. The girl was given a very strict talking to by the WPC but she was not charged with wasting police time, as she might well have been. It was left to her to tell her parents that she had just missed the last bus home and on starting to walk had been seen by a nice friendly copper, me, who was concerned about a young girl walking the streets at that time of night. The father thanked me and, together with his wife and daughter, left the station. As nobody suffered as a result of the false allegation, the girl quickly admitted to her lies, and given we did not tell the parents any untruths, I like to think we successfully averted what could have been a huge domestic confrontation.

Possibly one of the most harrowing incidents police officers have to deal with is serious fires, especially when loss of life is involved, and I was involved in two such cases when in uniform. The first involved an elderly man who lived alone and died when his bed clothes caught fire, probably caused by his smoking in bed and falling asleep. I was called by neighbours at about 2a.m., while on beat patrol, but the house was pretty much engulfed in flames and the fire brigade were unable to gain entry to the inferno. I later witnessed the charred remains of the poor man being removed from his house and they did not resemble anything like a human body. I later attended the post-mortem and coroner's inquest, which returned a verdict of accidental death.

The second death I was involved in was that of an alcoholic vagrant who lived rough on a bombsite in Stepney, along with several others who survived in a similar way. There were about six of them, male and female, and as usual were completely drunk on cheap alcohol and methylated spirit, all huddled around a fire. One of the sad souls fell head first into the fire setting his clothes alight and, although he was dragged from the flames by his drinking pals, suffered horrendous burns from which he died three days later. I took witness statements from two of the group and, again, the coroner's inquest verdict was accidental death.

On the lighter side, one of the funniest incidents I experienced while walking the streets of East London involved an alcoholic and his determination to get hold of a bottle of wine.

As I was walking slowly along Salmon Lane in Stepney, sometime after midnight, and "shaking hands" with shop door handles to make sure the owners had locked up — I actually nearly fell in a shop one night that had not been locked up — I noticed an unusual sight: a pair of legs sticking out from a shop doorway. The chemist shop had two large display windows on either side of the inset doorway, each one stretching to the ground and one with a letter box cut into the glass and located about eighteen inches from the ground.

As I got nearer to the doorway I saw that a man was lying on his side and he appeared to be drinking from the neck of a bottle that was sticking out of the letter

100

box. He was fairly drunk, not legless, but despite this he was one of the most ingenious thieves I ever met.

He was a self-confessed alcoholic and had been drinking in a local pub until it had closed. Deciding that he had not drunk enough, he had walked the streets looking for something to quench his desire when he spotted a bottle of wine on display in the chemist's shop window, fairly near to the letter box but not within his reach. Now, the shop was near a building site where the man found a piece of wire and a length of twine. He cleverly made a small lasso with the twine, tied it to the wire and returned to the shop doorway. The thief poked the wire through the letterbox and managed to loop the twine lasso over the neck of the wine bottle and with a tug had control of it. Problem: how to get a bottle of wine through a small letter box? No problem if you are an alcoholic in desperate need of a drink. He lay on his side, carefully pulled the neck of the wine bottle through the letter box, unscrewed the top and started to drink the contents. He had drunk about half when he noticed a big pair of policeman's boots next to him.

The irony of this was that the wine the thief was drinking was Sanatogen, Tonic Wine which was a health drink! On being told this he was most upset but, although I arrested him, I think he was proud of his exploits.

One of the most unusual arrests I made in uniform happened when I was on Night Duty. It was strange not because of the perpetrator of the crime but because of the weapon that he used. It was a very cold night, had been snowing for some time and there was a lot of ice about. I was informed by a member of the public that there was a fight in East India Dock Road and I made my way there. Two men were fighting, or rather, one was threatening the other with a strange looking weapon — an icicle. It was quite thick, pointed at one end and about eighteen inches long. The assailant had broken it off from a line of metal railings. The man being threatened said the pair were having an argument over a woman and he wanted the other charged with threatening to stab him with the icicle. I took the weapon off the man but when told he was being arrested he refused to let go of the railings. A swift crack across his knuckles from my rubber torch solved that problem and all three of us walked the short distance to Limehouse nick, me holding on to the prisoner with one hand and clutching the weapon in the other.

Just a routine arrest really, but I now had the problem of preserving the evidence, the icicle, for possible production at court and so, using my initiative, I put it in the police canteen food freezer. The station sergeant suggested that should the prisoner plead not guilty at court and the magistrate wished to see the icicle, then the SOCO (Scenes of Crime Officer) could be contacted to photograph it. That proved not to be necessary as the accused man appeared at court the next morning, pleaded guilty to the charge of being in possession of an offensive weapon, and was fined. That incident proved the point that just about anything can be used as an offensive weapon.

As a beat constable I quickly learned to expect the unexpected and this came about after I arrested a man for burglary. I was on Night Duty and patrolling my beat, which included a number of shops with goods entrances at their rear, which were accessed by a side alleyway. At about 2a.m., I noticed a man coming out of the alleyway into the main road carrying a television set. I recognized him as a person I had previously arrested for shop breaking and asked him for an explanation. His reply was "OK, I suppose I am bang to rights." I gave him the official caution, arrested him, and took him back to the station, with him carrying the television. A subsequent search with other officers at the back of the shops revealed that a television and electrical shop had been broken into and, on arrival at the scene, the shopkeeper confirmed that a television had in fact been stolen. When charged, the burglar said words to the effect that he thought he might be liable to get another six months in prison.

I prepared my witness statement for the CID officer who took charge of the case and we assumed that the shop breaker would plead guilty at court and quick justice would duly follow. How wrong we were, because when he appeared at the Inner London Sessions he pleaded not guilty and elected to stand trial before a jury, which was, of course, his prerogative. After giving my evidence of the circumstances of his arrest, the only thing the defence counsel questioned me on was the statement made by his client when I arrested him and which I was quite clear he had said. I was not allowed to repeat the comment he had made when charged as it

103

would have indicated to the jury that he had previous convictions. My prisoner, let's call him "Billy Liar", then proceeded to give evidence in his defence and as I listened I thought I was hearing something out of *Alice in Wonderland*; in fact I began to wonder if I was in the right court!

He told the jury that on the night in question he had been at his girlfriend's house and was on his way home when he wanted to have a pee. He knew it would be wrong to relieve himself in the street and so he walked down the alleyway and round to the back of the shops where he noticed that the back door of the television shop had been broken into. He said that he knew the owner of the premises to be quite elderly and he felt sorry for him. On seeing a TV set lying near the back door, good natured "Billy" decided to take possession of it and was on his way to the police station to hand it in when he was wrongfully arrested by me. When cross-examined by our prosecution barrister as to why he at no stage gave that explanation when arrested or charged with burglary he said, "Because I had a right to remain silent and, in any case, I thought nobody would believe me." Damn right we wouldn't.

The jury was not told, as is the general rule in English Law, that the poor "Good Samaritan" I had arrested had numerous convictions for various offences, including house and shop breaking, and had only just been released from prison. Still, it took them all of fifteen minutes to return a verdict of guilty and the prediction he had made when charged was half correct; the judge sentenced him to not six, but twelve months in prison. I was standing next to the dock as "Billy Liar" was taken to the cells and he leaned towards me and said, "Well, I had to have a go, didn't I? No hard feelings, eh?" At least he had a sense of humour and had attempted to use our legal system to his advantage, which he was entitled to do. I suppose I would put him in the category of a "likeable rogue".

One other amusing incident that occurred involved assisting the CID and getting a flavour for the type of work they did, it also probably partly influenced me in later joining that department. A detective sergeant, I'll call him Nev, had information that a team of four local villains was going to break into a television and electrical shop in Stepney. Everything was planned for a team of three detectives, assisted by four officers in uniform, to park up in police non-descript vans very close to the intended target premises, and when the villains were loading up their vehicle with stolen goods we were to burst out of the back of our vehicles and arrest them.

The information we had was quite good but we did not have the exact date of the intended crime and actually sat for two nights, cooped up in our vehicles for several hours at a time, which showed me that CID work was not as glamorous as some might think. It was the summertime and hot, the vans had little ventilation, we were unable to get out to relieve ourselves, so had to lift up a flap in the floor of the vehicle. Sweaty coppers enclosed in those conditions was not to be recommended.

However, on the third night the job was on. We were parked up and at about 1.30a.m. the villains arrived, stopping their large van with its rear doors only about ten feet away from the rear doors of the CID officers' police vehicle. We were parked on the opposite side of the road. We observed the criminals breaking the display window of the shop, enter and start to come out and load television sets into the back of their van. We were in radio contact with the CID officers, and when they gave the signal, we burst out of our van and rushed across the road to arrest the villains.

At the same time, the CID lads burst open the doors of their van but were hampered somewhat in getting out because the criminals had parked so close, and their rear doors were open for the loading of the TVs. The result was general mayhem, with both uniformed and CID officers chasing and attempting to arrest the fleeing perpetrators. We managed to arrest three, however, I will not forget poor Nev going to grab the fourth who was carrying a television set which he threw at him, or the sound of it smashing as it crashed on the pavement. The rest of us were all occupied with detaining our prisoners and unable to do anything except watch Nev's man disappear up the darkened street. Anyway, three out of four wasn't a bad haul and Nev loved telling anyone who would listen how good he was at sidestepping a flying television set!

Several years later, Nev arrested a man who told him he was the fourth villain and had thrown the TV set at him. Nev asked him where he had disappeared to that night. It turns out he had shinned up a lamppost and watched the whole episode, including the search for him, from on high! Nobody was able to identify the culprit so he was not charged with the breaking. Well, you win some, you lose some.

During my service I worked with several very good women officers both in uniform and plain clothes. They were extremely helpful when dealing with young children, indecent assaults and allegations of rape. One woman detective constable, Carole, told me a story that happened to her when she was attached to a squad in West London. Several prostitutes had been seriously assaulted and it was feared that eventually one would be killed. A squad was set up that involved a large number of women police officers patrolling the streets around Notting Hill and Shepherds Bush late at night, hoping to flush out the attacker. Carole told me that one particular evening a man had approached saying that he did not want sex, only for her to get in a taxi cab with him and drive round for half an hour while he took the knee-length boots she was wearing on and off her. Evidently he was prepared to pay pretty good money for the privilege and Carole said she was half tempted to accept the offer. Of course she didn't, the women officers were not allowed to get in any vehicle with a "punter". She identified herself to him, recorded all his details and added them to the investigation.

During my time in uniform I called for the dog handlers' services on several occasions, such as tracking down escaped suspect burglars. I can't recall getting any results from them but they were highly skilled — although they used some techniques that might not be approved of today.

Once when having refreshments in the canteen at Limehouse I witnessed an occurrence with a dog handler and his large police dog. The handler was sitting at a table having his lunch with his faithful animal lying at his feet. Another officer offered the animal a snack of some sort, which it happily accepted. His handler snatched the food from his dog, shouted at him and slapped him very hard across the face several times, causing him to cower down and yelp. The handler explained to his colleague that his animal, which was a very big German Shepherd, had been trained not to take food from anyone except him, the danger being that the food could be poisoned. He went on to say that police dogs were trained with kindness not violence but his animal was big and if it did wrong a slap across its backside, which probably most owners might do, would not even be felt. Yet it had to physically feel that it had done wrong, after all, both of them relied on each other so much that at times their lives might be at risk.

Police dogs could generally be stroked and petted by officers other than their handlers but I was always wary of them if I was in plain clothes. I once called for the help of a police dog when not in uniform and stupidly opened the back door of the van instead of leaving it to the handler. The snarling animal leaped at me. Luckily it was on a leash and unable to jump out of the van, but as I stepped back our faces were about a foot apart! The dog handler just laughed — lesson learned.

CHAPTER
SIX

Jokers in the Pack

It is not unusual for people working in stressful jobs — particularly where they are dealing daily with intense situations whether emotional, physical or mental — to have a sense of humour somewhat different to the general public, who sometimes find this strange and difficult to understand. Anyone working in such professions will tell you that their sense of humour enables them to carry out their jobs, and lack of it can cause depression. I have found servicemen, doctors, nurses, firemen, paramedics, morticians, funeral directors and even clergymen all, at times, come into this category. Policemen are no different, and during my service I frequently witnessed their humour ranging from practical jokes to the macabre.

When I arrived at Limehouse Police Station in 1961 I very quickly learned to be alert to the practical jokers on my relief who took great delight in picking on new constables.

Richard Green was a nineteenth-century ship owner and philanthropist who lived in Poplar. During his life he was responsible for the revival of shipping in East London; he also founded a sailors' home, a hospital and an orphanage. Green always took his beloved dog with him wherever he went and three years after his death in 1863, a statue of him and his dog was erected in East India Dock Road, outside the Poplar Public Baths. A few days after I began duty at Limehouse, I was told to go the Poplar Baths and meet a Mr Green, who could be identified as he had his dog with him, because he had some information to give about a crime. I duly went to the location, waited outside the baths and stood fairly close to the statue. It took about five minutes for me to glance up and notice the name on the plinth, "Mr Green", and the dog sitting by his side. So much for observation.

Another joke that was often played was for the telephonist to give a message to a raw officer for him to phone a certain telephone number and ask for a "Mr Lion". A stupid pathetic joke that must have driven London Zoo mad!

One colleague on the relief, Matty, seemed to be a frequent target for the practical jokers, although there was never any bullying — in fact he always saw the funny side of the prank and often gave as good as he got.

He lived in the section house and it was quite usual for us to socialize in each others' rooms. When we gathered in the parade room prior to each tour of duty we had to carry our appointments, truncheon, whistle, etc., and not put them in our pockets until instructed to do so just prior to going out on the streets. The truncheon was placed in a long thin pocket, next to the normal pocket, down and inside the right trouser leg.

110

One particular evening two or three of us were gathered in Matty's room prior to our Early Turn the next morning. He left for a few minutes to make a phone call to his girlfriend, and while he was gone one of our group noticed his uniform hanging up ready and thought it a good idea to cut the bottom off his truncheon pocket!

The early relief paraded the next morning, and following the usual information being given by the station sergeant and the beats allocated, the order was given to show our appointments and then put them away. We all did so, but as Matty put his truncheon in its pocket there was a loud thump as it fell straight through onto the concrete floor.

"Stop pissing about, PC Bryant, pick up your weapon and put it where it belongs," yelled the station sergeant.

Matty duly obeyed, thinking he had inadvertently missed his truncheon pocket, but again, a loud thud.

"You stupid idiot, PC Bryant! Is 5.45 too early in the morning for you? Just get yourself sorted out before you let yourself loose on the poor public!"

There was a lot of muffled laughter from the rest of us, particularly those who knew of the practical joke. Matty cursed his "sodding" friends when he realized what we had done and patrolled his beat that morning with his truncheon in his main trouser pocket.

It was possible for a constable to volunteer to become an official beat cyclist, for which they were paid a little extra in their wages and the only stipulation was that their cycle had to be in good working order, with working lights. During his tour of duty the officer would cover most of the six Limehouse beats. Matty was one of those officers and on one night duty, another of his colleagues, Chris, took the opportunity to play another practical joke on him.

In the station yard was a shed, in which were kept stolen or abandoned pedal cycles that had been recovered. Matty had returned to the station for his refreshment break and parked his bike in the yard. Chris had reason to go to the shed where the recovered stolen bikes were kept locked. He noticed a cycle that belonged to a local butcher, which had an advertising panel on the side and a metal basket on the front. Chris promptly swapped Matty's bike in the yard for the butcher's one and, on finishing his break, Matty went to pick up his cycle to continue on beat patrol. Not wanting to report the loss of his bike to the station sergeant, and realizing that his mates were responsible, Matty simply jumped on the butcher's bike, which had front and rear lights, and rode off down West India Dock Road. I am not sure what any local residents would have thought on seeing their friendly bobby on that bike but at least the butcher got some free advertising that night and the constable carried out his duty.

Another incident involving Matty Bryant happened one very wet and windy night. At about 2a.m. he phoned the station from a police box to report that he had heard noises coming from a building site and thought there might be thieves in the area. The police van duly arrived with the driver, myself and two other

PCs. Matty told us that he had heard noises but had seen nobody. The site was encased by scaffolding and the first thing we all noticed was the sound of clanging chains and creaking boards, quite usual for any building site during high winds and rain. The van driver told Matty to stay on the ground at the front below the scaffolding, myself and the others to cover the back and sides while he climbed up the ladders to the first floor of the building. It was dark and we were all using our torches. After a short while there was a huge crash as a scaffolding pole hurtled to the ground from the first floor and landed about six feet away from where Matty was standing. The van driver climbed down and denied all knowledge of the flying pole, suggesting it might have become loose in the high wind. Needless to say, no thieves were found on the site and we all returned to the nick for a nice cup of tea.

Although Matty was a good target for practical jokes he could also dish it out to others. One officer who arrived at Limehouse shortly after me, Andy Andrews, who became a good friend, was the victim of a hoax perpetrated on him not only by Matty and one other practical joker, but with the assistance of a sergeant, who was responsible for his ongoing training.

Andy was due to get married and on his day off had booked a meeting for himself and his fiancée with the vicar to finalize arrangements for the big day. The main method of inter-station communication was the teleprinter and Matty arranged with a friend of his at Arbour Square Divisional Headquarters for a telex-message to be sent to Andy, instructing him to attend

113

Arbour Square Police Station on the day of his meeting with the vicar, to undertake "whistle training". Andy was most indignant and told his sergeant that he had never heard of whistle training and he could not attend on that day anyway.

He was informed that a fairly recent directive had come into force whereby new officers were required to attend whistle training as it was important to know the various methods of using it to call for assistance and he would have to obey the instruction or he could be reprimanded. A number of us were in on the joke and told Andy we had all undergone the training, however, when he told his sergeant that he was going to make an appointment to see the superintendant at Limehouse the sergeant admitted to the hoax.

The first two or three nights of a tour of three weeks' Night Duty always seemed the worst as far as tiredness was concerned, but after that, once into a routine, I found it no problem to sleep during the day. However, one of my friends on the relief, named Doug Carpenter but always called Chippy, who also lived in the section house, was permanently tired and occasionally, towards the end of the night when he judged that everything on his beat was quiet, he would go back to his room and get an hour's sleep. He would usually tell one of his colleagues what he was doing and then get a call from them at 5.45 a.m. in order to report to the duty sergeant and book off duty.

One night, he forgot to tell any of us that he was going for a quick kip and as a result, when the rest of us left our beats and booked off, Chippy was nowhere to be seen. The sergeant, like the rest of us, was keen to get home to his bed, and by 6 o'clock became impatient and possibly a little concerned for Chippy's whereabouts and safety. After we had booked off, Dickie and I, guessing what had happened, went to Chippy's section house room and woke him up. Shocked when he saw the time Chippy went to rush to the station next door, which was connected to the section house without him having to go outside. Dickie stopped him and told him that it had been raining for the past hour and he couldn't book off with his uniform completely dry. Of course, this was a lie. Chippy promptly put on his raincoat and helmet and went and stood under the shower for about a minute until he was quite wet. He then rushed to book off, telling the irate sergeant, "All correct, Serge, sorry I'm late."

The latter took one look at the dripping wet constable and said, "Chippy, I daren't even ask, just fuck off!"

The winter of 1962–3, which became known as The Big Freeze and was the coldest since 1740, will always be remembered by those who experienced it. There were freezing temperatures and deep snow across the country, many communities were cut off and the nation more or less came to a standstill. It snowed on and off from December through to early March.

The East End of London did not escape, but the hardy cockneys got on with life as best they could. Schools were kept open as much as possible, shopkeepers and householders cleared their paths and neighbours looked out for each other, especially the elderly and vulnerable. I guess it was a little like the East Enders' wartime spirit.

We still carried out our beat patrols but often with difficulty, as in some places there were snow drifts up to four-feet deep. It was quite good fun though, particularly on Night Duty. The main thing was to keep warm, and several of us wore our pyjamas under our uniforms, which seemed to work quite well. I also wore two pairs of football socks. We were allowed to wear black scarves and permitted to return to the nick twice as often as normal for hot drinks. One also had to be alert during the night, when things on the manor were quiet, to suddenly being ambushed by colleagues with snowballs. This normally took place in the dark narrow streets of Limehouse around the warehouses but I think, in fact I hope, no members of the public witnessed our snowball fights. I also remember one particular night when it was snowing heavily and the streets were deserted, a colleague and I built a small snowman. Oh well, boys will be boys, however, we still did our job patrolling the beats and making sure the good citizens of Limehouse and Stepney could sleep safely in their beds.

One amusing story about jokes involved my wife, Anne, who I had married in 1964 — well, I thought it was fun! A colleague, John, and I were invited to a Boxing Charity Dinner in Central London and decided to change into our suits at work, leaving our uniforms in our lockers. After a very enjoyable evening I arrived home late and as I was leaving for work realized that I did not have my warrant card, which is an officer's official identification. I guessed that I had left it in my uniform the previous night and mentioned it to Anne. Losing one's warrant card was a serious breach of police regulations, and on travelling to work with John I expressed my concern. However, when I arrived I was relieved to find it in my locker.

John was without doubt one of the greatest practical jokers I have ever met and I always had to be on my guard and alert to his pranks; he knew Anne well and quickly seized on the opportunity. I was about to phone her and tell her that I had found my warrant card but, after ascertaining from me that our dustmen were due to empty the bins that day, John insisted that he rang her.

He told her that I was out on a job but had asked him to phone and inform her that I had not found the ID but I had remembered that on arriving home the previous night I had emptied my suit pockets and thrown some rubbish into the kitchen bin, the contents of which I had emptied into the dustbin. He told my unsuspecting wife that I had asked him to ask her to search through the dustbin. It was a very hot summer's day but my dutiful wife, assisted by a friend who was staying with us, put on a pair of rubber gloves, spread a plastic sheet out on our lawn, tipped the contents of the full dustbin out and the two of them spent about fifteen minutes sifting through the garbage! After half an hour

I phoned Anne to check John had told her I'd found my ID . . . her reply is not to be repeated here.

One tale about a very good friend of mine, Dev, happened when he was rushed to hospital and successfully operated on for a perforated appendix. Nothing very funny about that, you might think, but what subsequently happened was considered by some as amusing.

In the 1960s the Metropolitan Police had a convalescent home in Brighton on the South Coast, the purpose of which was to allow officers to recuperate from illnesses, injuries, mental difficulties or any other condition. After his operation, Dev was a perfect candidate and he happily went down to Brighton to enjoy the benefits of the bracing sea air. I visited him when he was there and he described to me the rules of the home, which he thought draconian, and which were enforced by the very stern matron. With the pubs and clubs of Brighton nearby, Dev had no intention of being locked up in barracks at 9p.m., and he soon found a way to break back in. However, one night he was caught by the night duty security officer, reported and given a warning.

Dev was determined if nothing else, and during his seaside sojourn met a local lady who obviously was not short of money and owned a sports car. He was the envy of the other patients as she picked him up each day, took him for meals, to clubs and race meetings then returned him, usually well inebriated, to what he described as Brighton's equivalent to Colditz. Everything

118

was fine until Dev's lady friend was found in his room in the early hours of the morning — one can only assume they were not playing Scrabble! He was told to immediately pack his bags and leave.

Shortly after that my friend returned to duty, but not before he was called in to see his superintendent, who had received a report of Dev's exploits in Brighton. The senior officer delivered a fairly mild rebuke but added that Dev could feel somewhat proud of himself as he was the first officer to have been instantly dismissed from the convalescent home. He was, but unfortunately he was married and his wife certainly didn't see the funny side when she found out.

Finally, a story involving another colleague, which myself and his other friends thought funny but he definitely didn't; I'll call him Mike to save his blushes. He was having an affair with a married woman and one night, when Mike was off duty and her husband was, apparently, working, Mike called round to see her for a drink and anything else that was on offer. The pair ended up in the bedroom and were enjoying the pleasures of the flesh when a noise downstairs announced the early arrival home of the woman's husband. Panic! Mike put on his clothes as quickly as he could but did not have time to get on his socks and shoes; he just grabbed them, opened the bedroom window and jumped. He later told us that he considered the risk was better than meeting the husband, and he had hoped to land on a flowerbed. Unfortunately he missed the flowerbed and landed on a concrete path, resulting in a broken ankle and a bad cut to the other foot. He managed to get to his car and drove to the nearest hospital.

When asked by the nurse in the Accident and Emergency unit how the injuries had occurred, he told her that he was a plain clothes police officer and had fallen off a warehouse roof while chasing a burglar.

"You normally chase burglars over roofs in bare feet, do you?" she replied.

However, she treated Mike's injuries, which resulted in him being off work for two weeks and also, because of his attempt at flying, getting the nickname of Batman.

All professions have jokers and the police are no exception. I met and worked with many and was happy to have done so.

CHAPTER SEVEN

Special Duties

Nineteen sixty-two was a year of general instability and unrest for the British people. The Cold War between the communist Soviet Union under President Khrushchev and the United States of America under President Kennedy had been building up over a number of years. In 1962 events came to a head with the thirteen-day conflict involving the Soviet Union, the USA and Cuba. It brought the world the closest it has ever been to World War Three with the possibility of the Cold War turning into a nuclear war. Across the world demonstrations, some quite violent, took place to protest against the political situation, and London was no exception.

During the Easter weekend of 1962, over 100,000 people marched to the Atomic Weapons Research Establishment, Aldermaston, Berkshire and demonstrated against nuclear weapons. At the same time, thousands demonstrated in London.

All police leave was cancelled and our numbers were strengthened by officers from other forces. H Division officers were posted in and around Parliament Square, where the Ban-the-Bomb demonstration was generally

121

peaceful, although the one that took place in Grosvenor Square became quite violent.

The main objective of the demonstrators seemed to be to try and bring the capital to a standstill. They simply lay down in the road and refused to move when asked to do so. They were informed that they were breaking various Westminster by-laws and then arrested. It took at least two officers to arrest an offender as they made their bodies a limp deadweight and some linked arms. They were taken to waiting police vehicles and transported to police stations around London, usually the one where their arresting officer was stationed.

My position in Parliament Square was at the junction with the Embankment and Westminster Bridge. The demonstrators, who came from all walks of life and sections of the community, were told via loudspeakers to clear the road and, on ignoring the instruction, the police were ordered to move in and remove them.

I walked forward to a group lying in the road, bent down and asked a middle-aged man to move. He did not speak to me. I again asked him to get up and told him he would be arrested if he did not. He still ignored me, I cautioned him and arrested him. His body remained completely limp but one of my colleagues helped me drag him out of the road and get him into a police van. After a short time the vehicle was full with officers and their prisoners and we went back to the East End to Leman Street Police Station — the cells at Limehouse were full by then. On arrival, all prisoners — there were about six — were put in the charge room in order to be processed. My prisoner, like the others, refused to give his name or any personal details, although he said he was a solicitor. Refusing to give a name or address meant that a prisoner would not be given bail.

Near Leman Street Police Station was a bombsite that had not been completely cleared or built on since the war. It was a permanent meeting place for homeless drunks, most of whom drank methylated spirits as well as other types of alcohol. Those sad people, men and women, would stop at nothing to get some form of intoxication, and I once arrested one such character who went into Boots and started to drink from a bottle of aftershave lotion that contained a small amount of alcohol. The down and outs would spend their days huddled around a fire, wasting their lives away.

Every few weeks police officers, usually acting on a complaint from the public, would go to the site and arrest most of the men and women for public order offences. They would be taken to the police station, which presented several problems to the officers on duty. Those arrested were invariably very drunk and incoherent, also filthy dirty with soiled clothes, smelled absolutely rank and many had head lice. When they appeared at court the following day, the odours were not welcomed by the court staff, but sympathy was usually shown by the magistrate, who sentenced drunks to seven days in prison as they had no money to pay fines. While serving their sentence, the prisoners would receive their first good meals for weeks, were de-loused and cleaned up, examined by a doctor and a chiropodist and treated accordingly. After seven days they would be given a new set of clothes, a small sum of money and then released to continue their way of life on the bombsite.

Prior to us arriving at Leman Street Police Station on Easter Monday with our prisoners from Parliament Square, the station officer — or possibly some other senior officer — decided that it was a good day for those who had not gone on duty at the demonstration to go and arrest about eight characters from the bombsite, who had been abusive and threatening to passers-by. The station officer was adamant that he did not know at the time that the cells were going to be used for demonstrators from the West End demonstration, but few of us believed him and decided it was his rather clever way of dealing with a logistical problem.

The arrested demonstrators found themselves in the charge room together with what can only be described as a bunch of stinking abusive drunks. Not only that, but they had to share cells with them. Needless to say, it didn't take long for the prisoners from the Ban-the-Bomb demonstration to remember their names and addresses in order that they could be verified and released on bail. My prisoner was one of them and a few days later appeared at court and was given a small fine.

The Easter weekend of 1962 was the start of months of tension and apprehension among the British public, due to the volatile political situation, and it culminated in October in violent protests in Grosvenor Square, an occasion when I was again on duty. The demonstrators were protesting about the Cuban crisis, and one objective was to gain entry to the American Embassy, which was then situated in the Square; the police's job was to link arms to form a cordon to prevent them from doing so. The whole atmosphere was something I had not previously experienced. The attitude of the crowd was very obviously one of violence, no doubt instigated by political activists. The American Embassy was deemed to be American territory and their troops, who were on duty inside, made it quite clear that it would be defended at all cost, and anyone who entered would be severely dealt with. They didn't succeed in entering the embassy, but several police officers, police horses and protestors were injured. Many arrests were made.

It was often necessary for police officers from several — or all — London divisions, and other forces around the country, to be used for duty at special events around the capital. These could be ceremonial events such as the Trooping of the Colour, or state visits of foreign heads of state, in addition to political demonstrations. Most of those duties were quite pleasurable and a change from the daily beat patrolling, others not so, and at times even frightening. If the duty was an official ceremonial one we were required to wear ceremonial uniform, which included a tunic with high collar, thick leather belt and white gloves. The outfit was uncomfortable, particularly on hot days.

The first ceremonial duty I was on was the Trooping of the Colour in 1963. We had to muster at Limehouse

Police Station at 6 a.m. and were taken by coach to Green Park, adjacent to The Mall in Central London. The weather was fine and hot and large crowds had already started to line the processional route from Buckingham Palace to Horse Guards Parade. We were given our position, which was halfway along The Mall, with the crowds, several deep, behind us. The procession was not due to leave the Palace until 10.30 a.m., and my colleagues and I passed the time chatting to the members of the public and, of course, being observant. I was surprised to learn that some of the crowd had been in position all night in order to get a good view. They had come from all parts of the country and there were vast numbers from other countries as well. Most were carrying Union flags, pictures of the Queen and other items showing support for the monarch.

The crowd was great and we were supplied with copious sweets and cold drinks. Two ladies I well remember from the north of England had a great sense of humour. They were standing immediately behind me and one turned to the other and in a thick northern accent commented, "Don't they make coppers short down here?!"

"Yes, that's because we don't get much rain down here in the south so we don't get watered much," I laughed. "Not like you lot up north where it never stops raining!"

"You cheeky monkey! Have another sweet."

Shortly after we took up our positions, a battalion of the Welsh Guards marched along The Mall and took up their positions immediately in front of the police officers. As they reached my position one of the guards, complete with rifle, stopped in front of me, turned, took several paces towards me — I was determined not to move — he stamped his feet and spun round so that his back was about six inches from my face. Me, five foot eight and this great brute at least eight foot five, including his bearskin, what chance had I got of seeing my Queen? Several of the crowd behind me laughed and the northern lady tapped me on the shoulder and said, "You could have done with a bit more rain couldn't you, mate?" I laughed and took a step to the side to get a better view.

Eventually, the procession from Buckingham Palace proceeded along The Mall with the great pageantry that only the British can do, led by a military band followed by the Queen on horseback and several open carriages carrying members of the royal family. As she approached, the cheering of the crowd grew louder, the flags waved and the guardsman in front of me stamped his foot and stood rigidly to attention. We had orders to be especially vigilant when the procession was on The Mall but I still managed to get a good view of Her Majesty. The ancient ceremony of the Trooping of the Colour took place on Horse Guards Parade, at the conclusion of which the Queen's procession returned to the Palace.

It was a long tiring day, and was the only time I carried out duty in uniform at the Trooping the Colour (I did so once when in the CID). I was proud to have taken part — albeit a very small part — in such a famous and historic event.

I only performed duty once on 5 November, in Trafalgar Square, and it was not a particularly pleasant experience. It was common practice in the 1960s for large crowds to gather in Central London on Bonfire Night and descend on the square, many of them drunk and armed with pocketfuls of fireworks. In those days, public firework displays were not as common as they are today and the fireworks not as sophisticated.

A lot of the male youths and troublemakers in the crowd seemed to take a great delight in throwing "bangers" and "jumping jacks" at people, especially the police officers. Ambulances were on standby and each year several members of the public and policemen were injured, some severely burned. One of my colleagues had a lucky escape when one idiot pushed his helmet up from behind and attempted to put a lighted firework in it. Luckily, the officer quickly ducked and it fell on the ground, whereupon the miscreant was arrested.

The job of the police was to control the crowd and keep any disturbances to a minimum. We had our usual powers of arrest and would carry them out if any serious offences were witnessed. It was, and still is, an offence to throw lighted fireworks in the street or any public place, and if we saw anyone doing so we could have arrested them; however, if we had arrested everyone we saw throwing fireworks, the numbers of police officers in Trafalgar Square would have very soon been greatly reduced, as they would have had to take the prisoners to police vans and away to be charged. Instead, we were allowed to use our discretion with the culprit and give them the option of being arrested or being searched and having any fireworks found in their possession confiscated. Obviously, everyone chose the latter, and we were supposed to take names and addresses, list the fireworks being taken and get them to sign our pocket books. This was not always possible as the general atmosphere in the square was somewhat tense and excitable — and it was fairly dark. Some people would simply hand over their fireworks and quickly disappear into the crowd.

The only pleasurable outcome of being on duty in Central London that night was that when we finally returned to Limehouse Police Station we had pocketfuls of fireworks that had been confiscated and not signed for. Those that had were deposited with the station sergeant, and those that weren't we were told to "just get rid of", which I am sure was not official police policy but I guess saved the sergeant a great deal of paperwork, as each firework would have had to be individually described and listed. I do know that it resulted in several of us, who had postponed our own bonfire parties with our families because of our duties, enjoying bumper parties the next day — well, we had to get rid of the confiscated fireworks somewhere!

On 31 December 1962 I was again on duty with other H Division officers in Trafalgar Square, which was a far better experience than that of Guy Fawkes Night.

In those days, Trafalgar Square was the place to be in London to see in the New Year. The whole atmosphere seemed to reflect the swinging sixties — the Beatles, free love and all that went with it — I seem to recall that there was a small fireworks display but nothing like the superb displays that we have today on the River Thames Embankment. The big highlight of the celebration was for the public to leave the pubs where they had spent the evening at about 11.30p.m. and descend on the square where, on the stroke of midnight, their main objective was to see how many of them could get into the fountains, which were left on. The public were not stopped from doing this and our duty was to make sure no crimes were committed and nobody was hurt. We police officers arrived in Trafalgar Square at about 9p.m., generally mingled with the crowd and enjoyed the tension as midnight approached. As the last ten seconds of the old year were counted out by the crowd and the sound of Big Ben struck midnight, a huge cheer erupted, those who were so inclined leaped into the fountains or climbed on to the huge lion statues and everyone hugged and wished each other a Happy New Year. We had been warned not to be too near the fountains at midnight as it had been known in previous years for some revellers to push officers in for a good soaking — all intended in the best possible taste, no doubt!

However, one very pleasurable part of the evening celebrations for us police officers was that several women seemed to want to kiss and wish a Happy New Year to as many of us as they could. Some were very

130

enthusiastic, to say the least, and it was amusing to see some of us lot covered in lipstick. Despite that enjoyable part of our duty, we still had to be alert for pickpockets operating in the crowds — and it was not unusual for some souvenir hunters to try and steal a police helmet.

The latter nearly caused a colleague of mine, Nick, to lose his job several years later. He had been in the Met for about two years in West London. He was not on duty on New Year's Eve but decided to go to the West End to celebrate with a few friends, one of whom was a solicitor. No doubt having had a fair amount to drink, they ended up in Trafalgar Square at midnight, after which they made their way home. On the tube train they met up with other revellers, one of whom had a police helmet in his bag which he sold to Nick for one pound. Unfortunately, on arriving at their destination, Hammersmith, Nick and his solicitor friend were confronted by a police constable who, on seeing the helmet, asked for an explanation. Nick explained how it had come into his possession but he was arrested for being in possession of stolen property, taken to the police station and charged with the offence.

Luckily, Nick was not in possession of his warrant card when arrested and just had his driving licence for identification. He had the presence of mind to realize the seriousness of his situation and did not say that he was a serving police officer. He was bailed to appear at magistrates' court the following morning and was represented by his solicitor friend who had been with him when the terrible crime was committed. Nick knew that he had no defence to knowingly being in possession of stolen property, although only he knew why he wanted the helmet as he had one of his own at home! The fact that he was a serving Metropolitan Police officer was not discovered, he pleaded guilty and his friendly solicitor addressed the court with mitigating circumstances as to his client's behaviour on a night of celebration. The magistrate was sympathetic and gave Nick a conditional discharge.

Nick left the police about two years after that escapade but he would undoubtedly have been dismissed if the facts had been discovered. In those days it was very rare for anyone with a criminal conviction to be allowed to serve in the Met — that is not always the situation today.

In 1968 I was on duty again in Grosvenor Square, in plain clothes during demonstrations against the Vietnam War and the British support for America. Our job was not to make arrests but to identify troublemakers and point them out to officers in uniform. There was a crowd estimated at over 25,000 and the situation was very dangerous for all involved as they broke through the police cordon and were charged by lines of police horses. Police dogs were also used and many officers were forced to use their truncheons. Stones, fire crackers and smoke bombs were thrown and marbles were thrown under the hooves of the horses causing several of them injuries. Two hundred arrests were made and fifty people hospitalized, some seriously, including twenty-five police officers. Those of us in plain clothes could do little and retreated to a safer side of Grosvenor Square. I can honestly say that was the only time I was really scared and concerned for my safety during my police service.

One of the advantages of being a member of the Metropolitan Police was, and has always been, that an officer will often be close to the action and quickly gain experience of various types of policing. I was lucky enough to have my fair share of the action and, although duty at public events often meant long hours and waiting around, it provided a break from the everyday work of patrolling the beat — not that that was ever dull.

I was on duty at several of Sir Oswald Moseley's public meetings in Bethnal Green. Moseley was the leader of the British Fascist Party, supported by his infamous Blackshirts. He usually held his meetings in or near predominantly Jewish areas of East London, but apart from some heckling, there was rarely any trouble, as by the early 1960s Moseley's support was dwindling.

Early in 1963, I had a rather more pleasant and relaxed duty at a cinema in the Mile End Road for the premier of a film called *Sparrows Can't Sing* starring Barbara Windsor. It was a film based on a stage play, which attempted to portray the life of typical East Enders, thus the chosen venue for the premiere. The atmosphere that night was somewhat different to those of the political meetings I had attended. The members of the crowd were all in a good mood and just wanted

133

to see and cheer their favourite celebrities as they walked down the red carpet. Notable attendees included Ron and Reggie Kray.

On another occasion, July 1967, I was again on duty in Greenwich when Sir Francis Chichester was knighted by the Queen following his circumnavigation of the globe in his small yacht *Gipsy Moth*. But probably the most moving public duty I took part in was on 30 January 1965, the funeral of Sir Winston Churchill. I was on duty at Tower Hill and witnessed the great man's coffin being taken on board the barge MV *Havengore* and commence the journey along the River Thames and on to his final resting place. It was quite a sight to see the Thames lined with thousands of people. London seemed to come to a standstill. Although working, it was indeed a privilege to have been there.

CHAPTER EIGHT

Sport

All my life I have been very keen on most sports, either playing or watching. The Metropolitan Police has always been a great organization for anyone wishing to participate in any number of sports. Most are played at police station, divisional, district and force levels, and several officers have come to represent the country at sports such as rugby, athletics and boxing. I found that, where possible, duties were arranged to allow one to take part. Each district had a sports club and excellent playing facilities. These were located at Bushy in Hertfordshire, Hayes in Kent, Imber Court in Surrey and Chigwell in Essex.

Musicians were also catered for. In fact, if they were selected for the Met Police Band they attended so many concerts, practices, etc., which counted as a tour of duty, that they rarely appeared at the stations to which they were attached. The band was of a high standard and played for many years at all of Arsenal's home football matches at Highbury Stadium.

At various times during my service I played several sports at station and divisional level — rugby, basketball (although I was a midget compared with the rest of the team), cricket, boxing, road walking, badminton and bowls. I also had regular games of squash with colleagues.

Each year, the Met Police held the British Police Road Walking Championship. This was a distance of thirty-three miles, which started at Barking and ended at Southend. It was an individual and team race and when I arrived at Limehouse I was informed that H Division had a very good record in the event. Being considered fit and young, in 1963 I was cajoled into joining the team and spent several off-duty hours training.

The race started at 9a.m. and was a particularly great day out for spectators. There were over a hundred competitors, a few of whom were of national standard. Numbers of public houses on the race route had special dispensation to open early and the many families and friends of the competitors travelled from pub to pub and cheered us on as we passed. Some of the less serious walkers, including myself, found time to pop into one or other of the "watering holes" for a quick pint and even a pie! The walk itself was gruelling, particularly the last stretch along Southend sea front, with the pier in the distance, which seemed to go on for ever. I did not exactly cover myself with glory but I was proud of completing the challenge, particularly considering the huge blisters I had suffered, finishing in approximately seven and a half hours. The H Division team came second. I took the next few days off to recuperate and Anne, who had supported me on the day, came with me to my parents' home in

Southampton. She spent most of the time putting her professional training to good use treating my blisters. Marrying a nurse definitely has its advantages.

I took part in the Barking to Southend walk on two other occasions several years later, representing the department at New Scotland Yard, where I was working at the time, pulling out with blisters the first time but finishing the second. Some people never learn, do they?

The Met has always boasted a very good force rugby team, which plays to a high standard. I had trials for the team but was not selected, however, I very much enjoyed playing rugby for H Division, having played at school and for Eastleigh Rugby Club. Our matches were played against other divisional sides and civilian teams. One would have thought that the most bruising encounters would be with the civvies, who'd want to put one over on the police. This wasn't the case, but our matches against other divisions were usually absolute wars, with inter-divisional rivalry coming to a head.

When I was a teenager in Southampton I joined the local boxing club and enjoyed training there twice a week. I had what I thought was a distinguished record of Fights 3, Won 1, Lost 2. I have a feeling that my sons get embarrassed when I talk about it, particularly my eldest, Steve, who was a fine amateur boxer. H Division had a good boxing team, with several members stationed at Limehouse. I joined the team and we trained regularly in the section house gym.

Each year the Met Police Divisional Boxing Championships for the LaFone Cup were held. The preliminary rounds were fought at Hendon Training School and at that time the finals took place at Seymour Hall in Central London. H Division always entered a team and we had boxers at several weights, the best of whom was Johnny Banham who I later worked with as an aid to CID. He was a light heavyweight, the same as me, but a much better boxer, and we sparred together often. Our manager decided that we should not enter two boxers in the same weight category and as Johnny had a better chance of winning the LaFone title than me at light heavyweight, I should enter as a heavyweight.

On the day of the preliminary fights at Hendon, Anne arranged to come with a friend and watch. As I recall, the heavyweight class was for boxers weighing about 12st 7lbs and anything over. I weighed-in and saw my opponent; he was a giant from A Division in the Westminster area of London, which generally only had officers six feet tall and above!

The first bell rang and I don't remember too much of what happened after that. King Kong came at me from the opposite corner, hit me and I landed on the canvas. At the referee's count of eight I got up, thinking I'd better put on a bit of a show. I clung on to my opponent and got warned for holding. I stepped back, was promptly smashed to the floor again, and got up hoping the referee would put an end to my suffering — but no such luck. Down I went again and as I started to stagger to my feet the referee put his arm around me and said, "OK, son, I think you've had enough."

You bet I had! I didn't object and suffered no injuries, just a large bruise under my left eye; I guess it was just my pride that was hurt.

I had a shower and changed and at that point Anne and her friend arrived. I explained that I had lost my fight but had put up a very brave and creditable performance. I decided there and then to retire from the ring, which was probably a good decision. My only consolation was that King Kong not only annihilated me but also went on to win the heavyweight title.

I jokingly blamed Johnny Banham for my hammering but he won his first bout and at Seymour Hall I watched him win the light-heavyweight title. He later represented England on several occasions and ultimately captained our boxing team at the Commonwealth Games in Edinburgh in 1970, where he reached the quarter finals.

Several years later when I was in the CID, sport played a part in helping with some very difficult police work. It was a horrific case. Early one morning I went with my detective inspector to an address, where we saw on the living room floor the naked body of a young mother who had been badly beaten, sexually assaulted and killed. Her five-year-old daughter, who was profoundly deaf, had apparently slept upstairs during the attack on her mother. A murder squad was set up and I had the sad task of going to Maidstone Prison with the DI to break the news of the woman's murder to her husband, who was serving a sentence for robbery. Next, I attended the post-mortem. The investigation continued for a number of weeks and before long, another officer and I were instructed to go to a particular building site in South London and arrest a distant relative of the girl for murder. He was eventually convicted of the murder, served some of his sentence but was later acquitted on appeal.

When a murder occurs the first few hours of the investigation are crucial, the adrenalin kicks in and everyone on the squad works very long hours, gathering evidence, sometimes not going home for thirty-six or even forty-eight hours. As the investigation progresses the pressure lessens and — when a positive result is achieved and an arrest made — it is still necessary for the squad to continue with its work of interviewing witnesses, taking statements, listing exhibits and preparing the case for court. This continues for several weeks, however squad members are permitted to take days off on rota. This murder followed that pattern, and after several weeks someone suggested that for a little light relief we should form a football team and play a couple of the local pub teams, which turned out to be a godsend. We all thoroughly enjoyed the games, followed by drinks and refreshments provided by the pubs, and we returned to the casework with new vigour on Monday.

After one of the games, a member of the opposing team, a well-known local villain, we'll call him Scottie, who had convictions for robbery and assault, among other things, suggested to us that he would get together a team of his friends from the criminal world to give us a game. After some amusing negotiations we reached

140

agreement, but with a couple of conditions: first, all his team should have criminal records and have served prison sentences; second, they should not play the game with a "let's get the Old Bill" attitude — we had no intention of getting the hell kicked out of us.

The day was fixed, but on the day Scottie told us he had a problem. One of his players had several convictions but had not been to prison, only put on probation. We told him we would overlook his breach of contract and let the miscreant play. The game was played in a great spirit, Scottie even reprimanded one of his team for tackling too hard, and I think ended in a draw. We all had a drink together after the match and no doubt the grounds may have been laid for some of us to cultivate possible informers.

There was one slight catch though, the "Villains XI", as they called themselves, were not aware that the spectators on the touchlines were not only supporters watching them play football. In those days there was a department at New Scotland Yard called the Criminal Intelligence Unit, C11, whose job it was to gather and collate information on serious crime and criminals around London. They got to hear about our football match and turned up at the game in an undercover nondescript van and took photographs of some of our opponents; they evidently wanted some up-to-date ones for their files. Dirty tricks or what? Not really, just part of the cops and robbers game.

Following on from that game we organized a charity football match against a showbiz team which included such stars as Ed "Stewpot" Stewart, Bill Oddie from

The Goodies, Jess Conrad and "Diddy" David Hamilton, all well known in the show business world at that time. The game was followed by a dinner dance at the Royal Artillery Barracks, Woolwich, and I arranged for two West Ham footballers Alan Stephenson and Bobby Ferguson, the Scottish goalkeeper, to conduct a charity auction.

We had set up a trust fund for the daughter of the murdered woman for when she reached twenty-one years of age and the proceeds from the football match, dinner dance and auction raised, as I recall, about £5,000. At least some good came about following the horrific murder of that young woman. I often wondered what became of her little girl.

After those events I became quite friendly with Kevin O'Shea who organized all the showbiz team's charity matches, and he asked me to play a couple of times for them — heaven knows why as I was a rugby player, not much good at soccer and definitely not a showbiz personality. However, when I appeared for the team I was introduced as a scriptwriter for the television series *Z Cars*, which was a complete lie, but I had the privilege of playing alongside the likes of Rod Stewart. Yes, sport did play quite a part in my police life in several memorable ways.

CHAPTER NINE

Socializing

Being a young man, single, with a good job, wage and no responsibilities, living in London in the early 1960s was a great time to be alive. This was the era of the Beatles, rock and roll, Carnaby Street, coffee bars and frothy coffee. Although in a responsible and what some might call an "Establishment" profession, of which I was proud, myself and my friends took full advantage of the changing times in which we were living. I still kept in touch with my friends in Southampton and several had moved to find work in London. However, the majority of my friendships were forged among my work colleagues.

The hours we worked were ideal for enjoying a social life, except of course, Night Duty. After finishing an Early Turn, an afternoon nap was usually the order of the day, unless watching or playing sport, which left the evening free for going out to enjoy oneself. Among favourite places I often visited with friends was the 21's Coffee Bar in Old Compton Street, Soho, which became known as the Birthplace of Rock and Roll, where such stars as Tommy Steele were discovered. Others who could be seen performing included Cliff

Richard — always a favourite with the girls; the wonderful Joe Brown; and Screaming Lord Sutch — many people have forgotten he was a big rock "n" roll star in the 1960s, before his political career with the Monster Raving Looney Party. Skiffle music was also very popular then, of which I was a big fan, and I am proud to say that I have every record that Lonnie Donegan ever made — much to the amusement and derision of my children.

We would spend several hours listening to the groups, drinking frothy coffee and chatting up girls, which may seem a little tame to what the young folk do today, but the world has changed so much. Other regular haunts were Ronnie Scott's Jazz Club, where we saw Humphrey Lyttelton, Johnny Dankworth and Cleo Lane, and the 100 Club in Oxford Street, where I saw a young Lulu — with her group The Luvers they performed a song that was to become a huge hit, "Shout". She was just fifteen years old, tiny, but with a huge voice.

On Thursday evenings we would often go to the Lyceum Ballroom in the Strand, a great place for meeting the opposite sex. I couldn't dance then and I still can't, but a few drinks at the bar and a shuffle around the dance floor seemed to impress some girls — several of whom attracted me enough to give them a lift home to some far flung area of the capital (this was, of course, before I met Anne). I did meet a very nice Australian girl who had represented her country in swimming at an Olympic Games, although no lasting relationship developed.

In casual meetings, my friends and I very rarely divulged that we were police officers, we would make up stories about being trainee lawyers or accountants. I usually passed myself off as a merchant seaman, which was easy to do in view of my previous life. One of my mates had a great line when trying to impress a girl. As most people probably know, the slang term for being arrested is "having your collar felt" and for going to prison "doing porridge". My friend would tell the girl that he was a salesman and when asked what he sold he would reply, "Oh, I deal in felt collars and porridge," which they no doubt thought a strange combination. He would often then add, "I don't get paid much, but I am very good at it and have many satisfied customers!"

I passed my driving test just prior to joining the police and bought my first car. It was a Wolseley 444, which was, coincidently, the smaller version of the police patrol car, the Wolseley 6/90. It was very handy for socializing and, in addition to visiting the East End pubs, my friends and I would visit various pubs in and around outer London and even further afield. Summer months were great for spending evenings at riverside pubs in Richmond and Hampton Court or the Old Bull and Bush at Hampstead.

Late Turn duty curtailed our socializing a little, finishing as it did at 10p.m. However, the M1 motorway had opened in 1959 and was still quite a novelty, and on several occasions myself and a couple of friends would jump in my car just after finishing duty and drive up the motorway, which carried very light traffic at that time of night, to Watford Gap Services.

After a leisurely meal we would drive back to Limehouse, arriving at about 4a.m. then sleep until noon and get up to prepare for the next Late Turn.

Billingsgate fish market and Smithfield meat market were also favourite places we frequented when on Late Turn. They were a hive of interesting activity during the night and pubs in the area were legally open all night for the workers; also some of the cafes served the most amazing breakfasts a working man could wish to devour.

Another good meeting place we often visited late at night was the Cafe Des Artistes in Chelsea, and it was there that I met Jill. After a few weeks we were at a party and Jill dropped something of a bombshell on me. She told me that her parents had made her a Ward of Court, she had a baby who had been adopted and also that her father had recently paid for her to have an abortion. This was considered all quite shocking for the early 1960s. I met her parents several times and they were lovely people, but it soon became obvious to me that they thought a London policeman would be a great catch for their daughter. I felt that I was not ready to be hooked at that time, certainly not in that net, and our relationship petered out.

Policemen and nurses, nurses and policemen, a well-known combination and recipe for human bonding? Certainly many policemen marry nurses, which is hardly surprising considering what they have in common: stressful jobs dealing with the public, working unsociable hours and having good senses of humour. A number of my colleagues in the section house knew nurses not only from the local hospitals — The London, Poplar and Bow — but also from others such as Bart's, Charing Cross and St Thomas's. Often, word would go round that a party was taking place at a nurses' home on a particular evening and several of us would go along. Doctors recently out of medical school, pretty nubile single nurses and young policemen all relaxing and wanting to enjoy themselves; a perfect cocktail for dancing to the latest rock-and-roll music, plenty of drink and party games — some of which involved removing clothing. Yes, some of those parties were very memorable!

Little did I know that one particular party I went to with a couple of friends in about November 1962 would change my life forever, as it was there I met my future wife. I had already been to a few parties at the West London Hospital, Hammersmith, and in fact was going out with one of the nurses, Cathy, at the time. At that party, she introduced me to her best friend, Anne, a gorgeous brunette who I immediately fancied but who showed little interest in me — probably because I was with Cathy. A couple of weeks later I was at the hospital in Hammersmith visiting Cathy but we had a row, I can't remember what about, and decided to finish our relationship. Prior to leaving the nurses' home I bumped into Anne, told her Cathy and I had split up and asked her out, to which she agreed.

We both very quickly realized that it was love at first sight; six weeks later Anne agreed to be my wife and we became engaged. For the next fifteen months we saw each other as often as our duties would allow, and we

147

got married in Worthing on 4 April 1964. Unfortunately, my best man, Dickie, fell ill on the day but another colleague, John, stepped in at the last minute, and many of my police and Anne's nursing friends attended. We were both twenty-two years old, have now been happily married for forty-nine years and are proud of our four wonderful children. Anne continued nursing until her recent retirement.

I must also here mention my colleagues who gave me great support in 1965 when my father died suddenly, just three weeks before our first child, Steve, was born. And again in 1971 when our daughter, Joanne, died at only seven-and-a-half months old. Anne and I were so grateful for the love, sympathy and help we received during those sad times. Although grieving, I found my police work helped immensely. I felt so sorry for Anne when we lost our daughter. She had our two sons to look after and was not working at the time, whereas I had my police work in which to immerse myself. Anne always supported me throughout my police career. I often think that it's not easy being a copper's wife — for many reasons — and it takes a strong woman to support a husband in that profession. The divorce rate for police officers is high. I consider myself very lucky to have met Anne.

The main objective of the International Police Association (IPA) is to promote friendship and help among all serving and retired police officers in most countries across the world, particularly when members are travelling abroad. I joined the IPA shortly after becoming a beat constable in order to take part in a trip to Munich, Germany, for the famous Oktoberfest Beer Festival. This certainly made a pleasant, if somewhat hectic, five-day break from patrolling the streets of Limehouse.

There were about twenty of us, not all from H Division, and we travelled from London to Germany by train. Imagine our surprise when we arrived at Munich Railway Station and were met on the platform by the Munich Police Band, who struck up with our national anthem followed by the "Colonel Bogey March"! We thought that our accommodation was going to be at the local police barracks, however, our hosts decided that the police barracks were not good enough for us and we were put up in an army barracks.

Most people think that the Oktoberfest is primarily one big piss-up, well I can confirm that it is! The Fest opened with a huge procession and carnival, organized by the major German breweries. From then on, the beer flowed freely and even if one went to a cafe for a cup of coffee it was compulsory to first drink a free glass of specially brewed festival beer. Our evenings were spent in the huge beer tents with the fräuleins serving steins of beer and the "oom-pah-pah" bands, wearing their ridiculous lederhosen, following which we made our way back to the barracks. The problem was, each morning we were there various official visits had been organized for us and we had to get up fairly early, all with hangovers from the previous night. A full English breakfast was laid on for us but first of all we were given a glass of beer, which we were told would

149

set us up for the day — which I must admit seemed to work. The trouble was the official visits we had to attend. One was to the Mayor's Parlour at Munich Town Hall where, once again, beer was the order of the day. Two others were tours round breweries! We returned to the UK all totally worn out after our hectic trip to the Oktoberfest but ready to carry on with our beat patrols.

You might be wondering what this had to do with being a Police Constable in the East End of London. Well, there were some more serious visits. On one of the days we visited the Eagle's Nest at Berchtesgaden, which was used as Hitler's retreat during World War Two. Apart from the history attached to it, there were some breathtaking panoramic mountain views. After leaving there we visited the concentration camp at Dachau, which was the first concentration camp opened by the Nazis in 1933 and where over 30,000 people perished. As I walked through the entrance to the camp, which to this day has been preserved as a memorial to all those poor souls who died there, and saw the gas chambers and ovens in the crematoria, I could not help thinking of a Jewish shopkeeper I knew back in Limehouse.

Over a cup of tea one day, he'd told me how he had been brought to England in 1939 by his mother but his father and all other relatives had died in one or other of Hitler's death camps. Sometime later, when patrolling my beat back in Limehouse, I popped in to see the shopkeeper for another cup of tea and told him I had visited Dachau; he just said, "Thanks," and shook my hand. He was typical of many East End Jews who fled Germany and settled in that area but rarely spoke about their past.

CHAPTER
TEN

Plain Clothes Work and Joining the CID

All Metropolitan Police Officers were required to spend at least two years serving a supervised probationary period, most of which was spent in uniform patrolling the streets. On some occasions, plain clothes street patrols were carried out, for example if there was a particular spate of crimes in one area. Also during the probationary period, in addition to the various station duties, one could pass a radio operator's course and be posted to a divisional area car for a period, which I did. Those postings were not permanent and usually lasted for about three weeks, but they did give the officers more experience of police work and made a break from patrolling the beats.

An area car crew consisted of an experienced Class 1 driver, a radio operator and a plain clothes observer. Their duty was to respond to emergency radio calls from the information room at Scotland Yard, which could be of any nature, typically they might be domestic disputes, pub fights, fires or breaches of the peace; anything that might be the result of a 999 call from the public. They would also sometimes assist the traffic divisional officers at serious road accidents.

During my tours of duty on the area car, I worked with several excellent drivers and the adrenalin never failed to flow when a "shout" came through from the Yard, the siren and blue flashing light went on and the driver used his exceptional skill driving at safe but high speed to the incident. I recall two or three such drives when we identified stolen cars and gave chase. That was when the operator really used his skills, giving a running commentary on the radio open microphone to constantly give our position to other police cars in the area so that they might join the pursuit and hopefully assist in stopping the suspect vehicle. Today the "stinger" — a strip of spikes — is thrown across the road to burst the tyres of a vehicle being chased, but we had no such devices and had to rely on the skill of the police drivers. I had total faith in them and never felt at risk.

We stopped one stolen vehicle and arrested the driver and two passengers, we lost another car in traffic. One vehicle we pursued and stopped had been reported stolen several days earlier. We stopped it at the first opportunity and it was obvious that the driver was terrified. Yes, his car had been stolen but was recovered, he had just picked it up from Bethnal Green Police Station and was on his way home; the recovery had inadvertently not been recorded on the official records. The driver understood our actions in spotting and stopping his car but added that it was a pity we were not about when it was stolen.

153

I did a tour of duty with a very experienced area car driver named Bert, who could best be described as "long in the tooth". We received a shout to go to a railway footbridge in Bow where a man was threatening to throw himself off. When we arrived, a small crowd had gathered and the man was sitting on the bridge and facing the drop to the railway lines below. I got out of the car and was going to go on to the footbridge, however Bert told me and the other officer to stay at ground level and keep the onlookers away. He climbed the bridge steps and went up to the man threatening to jump. A few words appeared to be exchanged, whereupon the latter climbed to safety, Bert took his arm and they came down to the road. By this time, an ambulance had arrived and the man was taken to hospital.

When we returned to our car, I asked Bert how he had managed to talk the would-be suicide down. "Oh, I just said to him, 'Are you going to jump or shall I give you a shove? Stop pissing about and making a spectacle of yourself and get down.' He didn't argue, so we can now go off and get our grub!"

I don't know if Burt actually said that, I wouldn't have put it past him, to be honest. If he did, I am sure his method is not and has never been recommended in any book on psychology, but whatever he said did work.

I am all for using psychology when dealing with difficult people. At training school we were basically taught to use our common sense, experience and initiative — perhaps that was what Bert was doing —

however, today recruits are lectured on psychology which can only be a good thing.

Another experience I had when I was an observer in the area car happened when we were on night duty. At about 5 o'clock one morning, in Roman Road, Bethnal Green, we spotted a car — I think it was a Jaguar — with only one rear light on. Our knowledgeable driver immediately recognized the vehicle as that owned by Ronnie Kray. We decided to stop Ronnie, who was driving and was the only occupant, not particularly because of the broken rear light, but using it as an excuse to search his car. We overtook him and indicated for him to pull over and stop, which he did immediately. He told us that he was on his way home from his West End club to his mother's house in Vallence Road. I informed him that he had a defective rear light, which he said he would get fixed, then we told him we were going to search his car.

At that moment a man was walking past on the opposite pavement; he was carrying what looked like a small lunch bag, and was dressed in British Rail uniform, probably on his way to work. Ronnie shouted to the man and hailed him over to us, at which point Ron explained that we were about to search his car and he wanted the stranger to be a witness to make certain that we didn't plant anything in the vehicle. The man watched as we carried out the search inside the car and the boot and found nothing of any incriminating nature. Ronnie thanked him, and us for overlooking the traffic offence, and then drove off. Ronnie was certainly a very imposing figure — well-built, with a mane of dark hair. I often wondered what his "witness" felt about that night. Did he recognize Ron? Maybe not, but it was hard *not* to know the twins in those days.

That was the only time I met either of the Kray twins, although later, as a detective constable, I did have several dealings with some of their criminal associates and became aware of the violence that surrounded that group and their rivals in south London, run by Charlie and Eddie Richardson. I took a statement once from a South London villain who alleged that he had been "dealt" with by the Richardsons, who nailed him to the floor with six-inch nails — he showed me the scars on his kneecaps saying that he was crippled for life.

One modus operandi that I was told the Krays used was to get a publican to accept a quantity of stolen spirits and from then on force him to pay protection money or alternatively have his pub smashed up on a regular basis. It would be wrong to sanitize anything that either the Krays or the Richardsons did, and other officers who worked on cases involving them might tell a different story, however, what little I had to do with them and their associates showed that they did not terrorize average members of the public but only dished out retribution and violence to fellow criminals who crossed them.

One plain clothes duty that I loved was the attachment to the divisional Q car, which was an unmarked police car, the crew of which comprised an experienced Class

1 driver, a radio operator and an observer, none in uniform. The main duty of the Q car and crew was to patrol the division, deal with crimes being committed or recently having taken place, such as burglaries and thefts of or from cars, then detect and arrest the perpetrators, if found. Unlike the area car, the Q car crew would not deal with accidents or traffic offences. A great deal of time on the Q car was spent carrying out undercover observations on people, buildings, vehicles and various locations. As with all responses to messages from Scotland Yard, we never knew exactly what situation we would encounter.

This fact was tragically borne out on 12 August 1966, and I remember it well. I was the plain clothes observer in the H Division Q car. Several thefts of lorries and their loads had occurred from lorry parks in the East End and we were in a park near the Tower of London, keeping observation on a number of large vehicles.

At 3.15p.m. a message came over the car radio from the information room, giving the registration number of a car, the occupants of which had been involved in the killing of all three police officers carrying out duty in a Q car near Wormwood Scrubs Prison in West London. As more news came through, my two colleagues and I couldn't concentrate much on our job in hand. Instead, we talked about how police officers took the job for granted and how vulnerable we all were. This was in the days before such equipment as Tasers, pepper spray and anti-stab vests.

It transpired that the three officers involved near Wormwood Scrubs — Geoffrey Fox the Q car driver, and his colleagues Christopher Head and David Wombwell — had stopped a vehicle containing three suspects — John Duddy, John Witney and Harry Roberts — who were acting suspiciously near the prison. While questioning the men, all three officers were shot dead. Duddy and Witney were arrested very soon after the murders but Roberts went on the run and was eventually captured living rough in a wood. The murderers were convicted of the crimes and all sentenced to life imprisonment. The offences occurred just eight months after the abolition of the death sentence in this country and one can only conjecture as to whether the three would have been hanged had the penalty still been in force at the time. Most officers I knew, and the vast majority of the public, were outraged by the shootings and would have liked the perpetrators put to death.

I was made aware of an interesting postscript to that terrible event a couple of years later. A detective inspector I worked with at Leman Street Police Station had been an officer on the murder squad in 1966 and told me that when Duddy, Witney and, later, Roberts were arrested and interviewed, all officers on the case were told in no uncertain terms that not a hand should by laid on them; any officer who did so would be dismissed from the force. Naturally, feelings were running very high — after all, three colleagues had been murdered — but the investigating officers knew of the huge publicity surrounding the case and did not want to give the defence any reason for complaint or appeal.

At the end of one's probationary period an officer had the opportunity to specialize in some particular type of police work in which they were interested. The choice was varied and included traffic division, dog section, mounted branch, river police, special branch — who were usually recruited via the CID and fluent in a foreign language — and the criminal investigation department. Some officers chose to stay in uniform and remain as beat constables, take promotion or work in other departments, such as the child protection unit. Promotion was open to all after two years and was by way of exams up to the rank of inspector, after that it was via selection and interview.

From the start of my police service, perhaps even before, the CID appealed to me and, if I am honest, I guess the so-called "glamour" of it, as portrayed on films and in the media, probably had something to do with it; they might not admit it but I think all officers who serve in the CID are attracted to it at some stage for the same reason. However, I would add that once joining the department one soon finds little glamour attached.

So, shortly after completing my probationary period, I applied to join the CID. Before becoming a detective it was necessary to spend some time, usually at least two years or more often longer, attached to the department as temporary detective constable or "aid" as we were known. I was interviewed by the detective inspector at Limehouse and, after convincing him that I would be a great "thief catcher", was appointed an aid, although still officially attached to the uniform section and liable to be called back into uniform to assist should any serious emergency — such as public order duty — occur. That never happened.

All aids worked in pairs, and the newly appointed ones teamed up with more experienced officers. My partner was Tony, who had been an aid for about eighteen months — he was an East End boy having been born in Stepney, and knew the area well, which proved to be a great help. Our duties were quite varied and covered any incidents involving the committal of crime. We worked shifts and spent the majority of our time patrolling the streets, as we had done while in uniform, but now in plain clothes and especially in areas where crime was prevalent. We patrolled all six Limehouse beats and used our initiative to watch or follow known suspects, etc. We dealt with anything from waiting for thieves to steal bottles of milk from doorsteps to keeping observation all night from inside and outside warehouses or other buildings, where we had information that break-ins might take place. Our job was to arrest criminals but not drunks or other minor miscreants. We were responsible for taking the criminals into custody, charging them with the particular offence, fingerprinting them, recording their antecedents, making notes of the offence and arrest, taking witness statements, where required, and attending court to give evidence — firstly the magistrates' and sometimes later at a higher court. As an aid, we worked closely with detectives at the station and often assisted them on cases. I was supervised by an experienced detective sergeant with whom I got on well.

A duty Tony and I always enjoyed was being posted to Petticoat Lane Market in Middlesex Street, Whitechapel, on a Sunday morning. As with all street markets, it attracts numbers of thieves, from pickpockets and scam artists to conmen. As patrolling police officers, our main job was to watch out for those undesirables and protect members of the public from them. One of the biggest problems was actually catching the offenders, as most were highly skilled at what they did and worked in teams.

One of the most difficult to catch were the ones that operated the Three Card Trick, or Find the Lady, as it was also known. All the team would operate with was just three cards, one of which was a queen. They would place the three face down, usually on an upturned orange box or on the pavement, and all the punter had to do was pick out the queen and win the money. The operators were so good that it was impossible for the poor unsuspecting gambler to win. It was an offence to play the game in the street and our job was to catch the offenders and arrest them. However, that was easier said than done: first, because the teams always made a point of identifying plain clothes coppers; second, there were only two of us; and, third, on a sign given by one of their lookouts they would disappear in all directions at the speed of light. It quickly became apparent to both the scam teams and us that we were all losers in that operation; the teams because they could not operate if we were around and kept hassling them and us because we could not arrest anyone because they constantly changed the one who actually played the cards.

We were under instructions to make arrests, which was pretty well impossible with these card sharps without other police assistance, which was not available. However, we did reach a compromise one week at the suggestion of one of the card team. He proposed that one of his cohorts who had run off on seeing Tony and me should surrender to us, be arrested and charged and plead guilty at court. The man arrested would have no previous convictions and thus get a small fine. Tony and I agreed to the deal, the scapegoat appeared, was arrested and everything went as agreed. Thus, we had our arrest, and the card team were no doubt able to continue to operate without interruption, at least from us, for an hour or so. Questionable police practice perhaps, but it was the 1960s and before the days of "big brother" watching from street cameras.

Leman Street Police Station frequently had complaints from irate members of the public saying they had been ripped off by the card gangs, although I had little sympathy for anyone stupid enough to risk their money with them. One particular complainant I saw turned out to be a police cadet from Hendon Training School! I pointed out the error of his ways and he agreed to withdraw his complaint.

Pickpockets, who included some young children, probably with a "Fagan" somewhere in the background, were another problem in the market. "Dip teams" were considered by us more of a threat to the public than the "three card teams". Anyone who was a victim of the dip team lost their possessions usually through no fault of their own, whereas mugs who played Find the Lady did it through choice. To combat the pickpockets, plain clothes police teams would work in the market from time to time, often with quite good results.

While attached to the CID as an aid I had an experience that affected me greatly at the time — and still saddens me today when I think of it.

It happened shortly after I was appointed an aid and paired up with Tony. We spent many hours patrolling the streets and one lunchtime, we called in to Leman Street Police Station for our refreshment break. When we had finished, Tony told me to remain there as he was going out for a few minutes to do some shopping.

After about ten minutes he returned and we continued our street patrol. As we walked, Tony asked me if I would do him a favour. "Will you go to your bank and say that you have signed a cheque?" he asked. I asked him what on earth he was talking about and he said, "I tried to cash a cheque at your bank and they just want you to verify that it's OK."

"Tony, what the hell are you talking about?" I asked.

"I took a cheque out of your cheque book," he explained. "When we were in the car a few days ago

163

and I signed your signature and tried to cash it at your bank. The manager wants to talk to you about it."

My bank was in Aldgate, and as we walked the short distance there I was in a total state of shock. I knew that Tony always seemed short of money but I really could not comprehend exactly what he had done or was telling me. As we arrived at the bank, the manager was standing on the steps and ushered us inside.

We sat down in his office, whereupon he showed me a cheque that had the words "Cash" and "Thirty pounds" written on it. It also had a signature purporting to be mine but which was nothing like it — in fact it didn't look as if any attempt had been made to make it look like my signature. "Is this your cheque?" the manager asked me. I said that it was and the manager continued, "And is this your signature?" I confirmed that it definitely was not.

I produced my cheque book and from the number on the forged cheque it was confirmed that it had been taken from the middle of the book. The manager told Tony to leave his office for a short while, and explained to me that my colleague had tried to cash the cheque at the counter but had been refused for two reasons — first, the cashier knew me and was highly suspicious of the signature, and second, unbeknown to Tony, my account was already at my overdraft limit and even if the cheque had been genuine it would not have been possible to cash it. The manager asked me if I was going to report the matter to my senior officers and I told him that I was in such a state of shock that I really did not know, I needed time to think about what I should do.

He explained to me the bank's position and the action he was going to take. He said he was obligated to report the incident to his regional office who might, or might not, refer it to their fraud department. He went on to advise me that I should seriously consider reporting Tony's action to my superior officers, regardless of the consequences to Tony. If I did not and it later came to their notice via the bank, then it could be construed that we were both part of the fraud and had shared the thirty pounds between us. What I was told seemed to make perfect sense.

Tony and I left the bank at about 2p.m. and the next few hours were some of the worst of my life. If an unknown person had perpetrated the fraud then I would have had no hesitation in reporting the matter to the police. However, my predicament was different: Tony and I had worked together for about nine months and become friends and he was a good thief catcher. He and his wife had one or two small children, and my wife and I had become friends with them.

For the next couple of hours, Tony and I slowly walked from Aldgate back towards Limehouse and our minds certainly were not on the job. He spent the whole time pleading with me not to report him, at times he was in tears. He said how sorry and stupid he had been and he had only done it because he was short of money. He asked me to think of his wife and family and what they would do if he went to prison, as he probably would, if charged. As we walked we ended up outside the infants' school where his wife had just picked up his son. Tony kissed them both and said he would see them later. As we walked on and back to Limehouse he kept on pleading with me. I think I was probably as distraught as he was but in a different way.

We eventually arrived at the station and booked off duty at about 5 p.m. Tony wanted to stay with me but I told him I still hadn't decided as to what to do and told him to go home. I went to the canteen and, as I sat drinking tea, I contemplated my alternatives. If I reported Tony I knew that he would more than likely be charged with criminal offences, probably sent to prison and certainly dismissed from the police. He was popular with other colleagues and I thought that if I reported his offences I might be ostracized by other officers.

I had a very good friend who was an experienced detective sergeant, who also knew Tony well. I knew that he was on duty at Poplar Police Station, so I rang him and asked if I could see him. I went the short distance to Poplar, related the whole sad story to him and asked for his advice. He immediately said that I had no choice other than to report the matter. He totally agreed with what the bank manager had told me could happen, should I decide not to do so. The DS advised me not to let my heart rule my head and to leave the outcome to senior officers. He also assured me that I would not be looked upon badly by other colleagues when they heard the facts. My decision was made and my friend phoned our detective superintendent to inform him of the facts.

Within half an hour I was being interviewed by the detective superintendent, who was in no doubt that I had made the correct decision. I made a full witness statement but I insisted that in it I stated, "If it was my decision, I do not want Tony to be charged with any offences." Although the officer said he fully understood my feelings, the decision was not mine but ultimately that of the Metropolitan Police solicitors.

I arrived home very late that night and explained to Anne what had happened. Naturally, she was very shocked and neither of us got much sleep. At work the next morning I was given a new partner, Duncan, and as we walked the Limehouse beats we discussed what had happened; he also knew Tony well and had worked with him in the past. I had no repercussions from any of my colleagues, indeed many said they felt sorry for me and they would undoubtedly have done the same thing.

Tony was subsequently charged with the theft of my cheque, and other offences, but when he appeared at Thames Magistrates' Court, where he had given evidence as a police witness many times, he pleaded not guilty. I, of course, was the main witness and it was the one time in my police service when I hated giving evidence. I was cross-examined very little, Tony was found guilty and sentenced to six months' imprisonment. However, he immediately appealed and was given bail.

Eventually we had to go through the whole sorry exercise all over again and Tony stuck to his original, rather surprising, excuse for his actions. He said that he had no intention to steal any money from my account but that he had no faith in banks and he just wanted to prove that they made mistakes. He asked the court to believe that he was going to draw out the thirty pounds from one cashier, then immediately go to another cashier and pay it back into my account! His explanation was not believed and his original sentence was upheld.

My new partner Duncan went down to the cells to see Tony before he was taken to start his sentence. Duncan told me that Tony had asked him to tell me that he apologized for what he had done and that there were no hard feelings as far as he was concerned. Strange though it may seem, I think I felt the same and probably still do. I was so sorry for Tony's family because, to the best of my recollection, he was in prison for Christmas.

It's common knowledge that police officers who go to prison are often given a very hard time; many elect to serve their whole sentence in solitary confinement. I'm sure it wasn't easy for him. I heard that on his release, Tony decided to start a new life working in another part of the country. I hope he was able to put that one terrible mistake behind him and move on, and that he and his family have been able to live happy and successful lives.

We all go through life having to make choices; unfortunately Tony made the wrong one with tragic consequences. As a result, the predicament I found myself in presented me with one of the biggest decisions I had to make at that comparatively young age. Since then, I have had to make some huge choices throughout my life but I don't think any have affected others so much as this one did, to Tony and his family, when I was in the police.

I also felt quite sorry for one particular person I arrested while patrolling in plain clothes with a colleague. At about 11.30p.m. we were walking along West India Dock Road, only a short distance from the police station and not far from West India Dock Gate, when we noticed a man staggering towards us, obviously very drunk, and tossing a bottle from one hand to the other. We would normally have ignored him and let any of our patrolling beat PCs deal with him and arrest him for drunkenness, if they thought it necessary. However, because of his possible threat with the bottle, we decided to approach him. As we did so, he swung the bottle above his head and although Ross ducked he received a glancing blow to his temple, luckily causing no injury. We both grabbed the assailant, shouting at him that we were police officers, but he would not let go of the bottle and became quite violent. Ross pinned him against a wall and, as he did so, I drew my truncheon, a shorter one than that carried when in uniform, and hit the man across his hand, causing him to drop the bottle, which smashed on the ground. At that moment, two of our fellow uniformed officers came running from the station to assist us. Evidently a member of the public had gone into the nick and reported that two men were in the street beating up a man and using a cosh to do so! Ross and I arrested him and took him to the station, whereupon we discovered that our prisoner was a seaman from Poland who spoke no English. An interpreter was called and we ascertained that our seaman was returning to his ship in West India Dock after a night ashore. After the Pole had sobered up a little, he explained that he had quite an amount of money hidden in his socks, he had not realized we were police officers and when we approached him he thought that he was going to be robbed. Having experienced the dangers of getting drunk in foreign ports when I was a seaman I empathized with him. Ross had also served overseas in the army prior to joining the police and was similarly understanding of the seaman's actions. We discussed what had taken place and, in view of the fact that Ross was in no way injured by the blow to his temple, we agreed not to charge the man with assault on police or being in possession of an offensive weapon but just drunk and disorderly.

The next day the Polish seaman appeared at Thames Magistrates' Court and through his interpreter pleaded guilty to the charge and was given a small fine. Interestingly, after the court appearance he insisted that Ross and I went to a nearby pub with him and his interpreter where he bought us a drink, apologized for his behaviour and thanked us for the treatment he had received, adding that he would leave England with a good impression of the police. After exchanging some of our respective seafaring experiences he went back to join his ship. Another satisfied customer?

★ ★ ★

I learned a valuable lesson from another amusing incident when in plain clothes when a colleague, Steve, and I were deputed to travel by train to Scotland to escort a prisoner who had been arrested in Clydebank back to London to face trial. He was wanted on warrant at Limehouse for an offence of grievous bodily harm.

We had a relaxing enough journey to Glasgow, arriving in the early evening, and went on to Clydebank where we booked into our hotel. The two local CID officers who had detained our suspect picked us up and we insisted on taking them out for dinner on the Met Police Commissioner's expenses, after which they took us to see the sights of Clydebank, which consisted of viewing the inside of several pubs.

It was a few days after Christmas and before the New Year, all the pubs were decorated and in full swing, ready for Hogmanay, and everywhere we visited insisted we sampled their various types of whisky. Consequently, Steve and I didn't remember being delivered back to our hotel by our hosts.

Shortly after breakfast the following morning our two friendly officers arrived to take us to Clydebank Police Station, we thought it was to pick up our prisoner and return south but, oh no, although we had rail tickets booked, they changed them to a later train and informed Steve and I that they were taking us to see Loch Lomond and have lunch before leaving. As a result, we spent several hours seeing the beautiful sights of which the Scots are rightly so proud, followed by a large haggis meal and, of course a "wee dram" or two!

We then picked up our prisoner and were driven to Glasgow to get our train. The only personal property the prisoner had was a few pounds, which were given to him prior to being handed over to us. I handcuffed him to Steve before boarding the train, covering the cuffs with a coat so that the public could not see them and become aware of who their fellow traveller might be. We found our reserved compartment and gave him the option of being handcuffed to the overhead luggage rack — thus standing all the way to London — or behaving himself, having the cuffs removed and sitting in the seat furthest away from the door to the corridor. He, understandably, chose the latter. Our travelling companion was quite amiable during the journey, telling us about his family and that he knew he would be going to prison for the stabbing.

Some way through the trip, the effect of our over-indulgence the night before, and that day's heavy lunch, resulted in both Steve and I falling asleep. The train was due to wait at, I think, Crewe for about ten minutes and when it stopped we both woke up and immediately realized that our prisoner had gone and the door to the corridor was open. I remember thinking, 'Oh, shit, that's my police career over.' We both leaped up, got off the train and on to the platform, only to see our charge walking towards us from the direction of the station buffet and carrying three plastic cups. "I hope you don't mind," he explained. "But you both looked shattered and I thought you could do with a cup of coffee."

The rest of our journey was incident free and we escorted our prisoner back to Limehouse where he was charged with GBH, subsequently pleaded guilty and, as he had predicted, was sent to prison for twelve months.

I suppose the two lessons I learned from that episode were, firstly, the stories one hears about Scottish hospitality are absolutely true; and, secondly, some criminals *can* be trusted . . . sometimes! I did several other prisoner escorts during my service but none was quite as eventful as that trip to Clydebank.

When I was a detective at Leman Street, I was actually blamed for the escape of a prisoner, although I still categorically deny it. Two officers from Manchester had come to London with an arrest warrant for a man wanted by their force for fraud and who was also on the periphery of the Kray brothers' criminal activities. He evidently did not know he was being sought, because he was still living at home and, because I knew him from past dealings, I was instructed to go with the officers to identify him and assist with the arrest.

We went to his address, which was a first floor flat in a tower block, found him in with his wife and told him he was being arrested and going to be taken to Manchester. He was quite pleasant and asked if he could pack a small bag of clothes and toiletries to take with him. We agreed and I told the two other officers that I would go to the bedroom with their prisoner, suggesting that one of them came with me while the other stayed in the lounge with his wife. She offered to make us all a cup of tea to which we agreed but when she shouted to us in the bedroom, the Manchester officer, who had been standing by the partly open bedroom window, went back to join his colleague and the wife, presumably for his cup of tea.

A few seconds later the prisoner rushed across the bedroom to the window, pushed it wide open and jumped out. I looked out and, although there was grass below decided not to become a hero or an invalid. The last I saw of the escapee was him running into some nearby bushes. The other two officers and I chased down the stairs after him but found no trace, even after calling for a police dog to assist the search. He was eventually arrested about a year later.

The Manchester boys returned home without their man but several weeks later my detective superintendent received a letter of complaint from their senior officer totally blaming me for losing the prisoner. It was obvious from their statements that his officers had been somewhat economical with the truth, not wishing to take any responsibility — no mention of cups of tea! My boss just made a few disparaging remarks about Manchester Police being inferior to the Met and sent back a terse reply to the complaint. Throughout my service I always found that if one was honest with senior officers, especially when one might have used questionable tactics or bent the rules a little when dealing with difficult situations, then they would give good support and backing, albeit sometimes after a bollocking!

The Metropolitan Police Criminal Investigation Department was set up in 1878 by Howard Vincent and was originally responsible to the home secretary, but in 1888 it came under the authority of the commissioner of police.

After several years serving as a uniformed officer and then as an aid to CID, I passed the selection board and became a permanent member of the CID, and was appointed a detective constable. I had many happy years in that role, serving in East and South London, and at New Scotland Yard with the stolen motor vehicle branch, known as C10. I have many stories to tell of my experiences in the CID but they are perhaps for another time, however, I will briefly describe what the switch from uniform involved.

One big difference was that whereas the uniformed branch worked mainly eight-hour shifts and anything over that was paid overtime, in the CID we were paid more but had to work alternative shifts of eight hours one day followed by thirteen hours the next. Overtime was usually only paid if one worked on a specific squad.

We underwent a course at the Detective Training School in Chelsea, which involved many lectures and demonstrations on criminal investigation, techniques for interviewing suspects, fraud and many other subjects. It also included a visit to the Black Museum at Scotland Yard, which we had not been allowed to see as new recruits. The museum was opened in about 1875 and is now called the Crime Museum. We were shown numerous exhibits from famous crimes that had taken place, including the Jack the Ripper murders, Haigh the acid bath murderer and Christie the serial killer who was hanged in 1953 for murdering at least eight people. He kept the pubic hair of some of his female victims in matchboxes, which were on display.

Some exhibits were quite gory but fascinating, such as the death masks of prisoners who had been hanged at Newgate Prison. One particular exhibit that impressed me was a forged Swiss bank note — the character who had produced it was a man of about seventy-five years of age, who had served a term of imprisonment for his effort. The interesting thing about the forgery was that he had done it totally by hand and the design was extremely intricate and contained numerous colours. It was so good that it was nearly impossible to differentiate between a real note and a fake. The surprising thing was that the Swiss note the old man had painstakingly taken hours to forge had one of the lowest values of any Swiss bank note at that time and was worth very little. Forging any country's currency is of course a serious offence and therefore the offender went to prison. However, to my mind the sad thing about it was that he obviously had great artistic talent but used it for criminal purposes, instead of maybe using it to earn a living as an honest, possibly brilliant, artist.

A detective's job is obviously investigating and hopefully solving crimes, whereas that of a uniformed officer is to prevent crimes occurring, keep the public safe, along with a multitude of other tasks. I always believed the uniformed branch was the backbone of the Met Police and had great respect for them, but at a few police stations where I served there was a distinct feeling of "us and them" between the two branches. Some CID officers referred to their uniformed colleagues as "Wooden Tops", which I regarded as quite degrading. I prided myself in always getting on well with my uniformed colleagues and made a point of communicating with them and keeping them up to date with any investigation I was doing that involved them.

As a detective at C10 I travelled to many parts of the UK on investigations. The branch specialized mainly in the theft of all types of expensive vehicles, often including their export. I travelled to Scotland and Ireland, also to Paris where I worked with Interpol.

One particular job I worked on with six other officers had, coincidentally, a number of links to the East End of London. It involved the theft of Triumph motorbikes and parts and took over two years to investigate but it resulted in nineteen offenders being convicted at the Old Bailey for conspiracy and theft. During the investigation we went to the Annual Motor Cycle Show at Earls Court and took possession of two racing motorcycles that were on display and had stolen parts built into them. The owner had purchased them from a dealer in the East End of London. The second link with the East End appeared when we went to Bournemouth and, after requesting permission from the then chief constable of Dorset and Bournemouth Police, called in

177

all the forces' police motorcycles, examined them and, as a result, seized two that also had stolen parts built into them — the police had purchased them from the same dealer in the East End, unaware that they were stolen! All seven of us involved in that case received both the Old Bailey judge's and Met Police commissioner's commendations for our work and were rather sarcastically nicknamed "The Magnificent Seven" by our colleagues at C10.

A number of us at C10 did not want promotion, as we knew promotion to detective sergeant would mean a transfer, usually back to a CID office on division. I was "instructed" to take the promotion exam, did little study and of course failed, but achieved my objective of staying at C10, which most of us thought to be one of the best-kept secrets in the Met. One of my colleagues was reprimanded for writing nothing on his exam paper except his name! On reflection, this was rather a short-sighted attitude but I loved that posting and remained there for several years as a detective constable, in fact for my remaining years with the force.

CHAPTER ELEVEN

Informants

Dealing with informants has always been an important part of police work and all officers, whether uniformed or CID, rely on them in some way or other. There are basically three types of informant.

The first and probably most important is the ordinary member of the public with whom the bobby on the beat will come into contact on a daily basis. It could be someone calling in at a police station to give some small amount of information — such as traffic lights not working or an abandoned vehicle — which although seemingly trivial, is important for the good running of the local community.

This group also includes such people as shopkeepers, newspaper sellers and publicans who can be a mine of information when it comes to knowing what's going on in their area. It is so important for the beat copper to get to know those folk as soon as he comes to a station — a cup of tea every now and again is not necessarily skiving but promoting relationships between the police and public and can prove invaluable. A uniformed officer will not usually have specific informants, but over time, if he is a good beat officer, he will get to know his locals.

The second is similar to the first but one that an officer should be wary of. This is the person who just loves talking to a police officer in uniform — for whatever reason — and gives information that is usually of no value whatsoever. Sometimes it is done with no malice, but sometimes it is untrue and can even be malicious. These people are often lonely or mentally unstable, but it usually does not take an officer long to identify such folk. I found it best not to dismiss them out of hand but to humour them kindly and make them feel that the information they were giving was important. I recall one dear old lady who used to call in to Limehouse Police Station regularly with startling information such as her cat had disappeared for an hour the day before and she believed her neighbours had kidnapped it so that it could mate with their moggy. She was told to keep an eye on things and if her cat had kittens to let us know and we would "look into it for her". The dear old soul sometimes brought in a box of chocolates for the lads.

The third type of informant is a different kettle of fish all together, and one whom the handling officer should also be wary of — but for different reasons. Many detective stories and television police programmes have depicted informants in their various guises, much of which is pure fiction. However, in the real world such characters are vitally important in the fight against crime. I cultivated some of them in my time and, even though that's fifty years ago, looking back to the ways

180

they thought and the arrests I made because of the information they supplied gives an insight into those times and those people.

Informants are nearly always criminals themselves and are generally referred to as "grasses". The expression "honour among thieves" is probably the most important rule in the criminal fraternity, and anyone transgressing that is considered the lowest of the low and can expect severe retribution against them or their family if exposed. Therefore, for anyone to "turn grass" is not only very risky but also a huge decision to be made by an informant.

I quickly learned from more experienced officers the importance of trying to identify the reasons that an informant wanted to divulge information. There could be any number — financial gain by way of a reward, revenge, to receive a lesser sentence at court for some crime they may have participated in, or to avoid arrest for some crime that they have or are going to commit with others. There may be other reasons but, whatever they might have been, it was obvious that any handling officer had to be extremely careful when dealing with informants.

Unlike today, an officer would often not have to divulge the identity of his informant to anybody — including his colleagues and even senior officers — they were not expected to. I sometimes went on a police operation, such as a drugs raid, that took place as a result of a colleague receiving information from his informant, without ever knowing who that was. The system seemed to work well and we had some good results.

How did I get an informant? Well, whether as a uniform officer or a detective, the one thing I did *not* do was to say to a villain, "How would you like to be my informant?" It just did not work like that, informants have to be groomed over a period of time and an officer must decide if a possible candidate would be susceptible to such a suggestion. Something may be said to an officer at court that might give an indication that the criminal might want to become an informant but generally, in my day, the officer would frequent the places where criminals socialized — such as pubs, clubs and cafes — and get to know them, not covertly but quite openly as a police officer.

When I was an aid to CID we did visit such establishments but our main job was patrolling the beats. On being posted to a police station as a CID officer after leaving the uniformed branch, I quickly found that each detective "had their own pubs". Detectives made themselves unofficially responsible for particular public houses on the manor and would visit them pretty frequently, either alone or sometimes with a colleague, especially on a Late Duty, when they had finished investigations or paperwork and things were quiet.

One particular detective sergeant I worked with, I'll call him Ray, had a rather unusual way of working, as I found out at about 9p.m. one evening when we were on Late Duty. Things were quiet and we decided to spend the final hour of our shift at a respectable local pub, obviously letting the duty inspector at the station know where we were. We had just had the first sips of our pints when Ray received a call via the landlord's phone from the nick telling him that a villain he wanted for burglary was in another local pub. Ray had an arrest warrant for him in his in-tray, and so we quickly returned in the CID car to pick it up, along with a pair of handcuffs, and then went straight to arrest the wanted man. He offered no resistance and was put into our car.

I assumed we were going straight to the police station with the prisoner, however Ray had other ideas and told me to drive back to the pub we had left earlier. He told the villain that the necessity of having to go and arrest him had caused him to leave his pint of beer, which he thought an inconvenience to say the least! Ray did a deal with his prisoner, that if we all returned to the pub, Ray would not handcuff him but place him on a seat in a corner between the two of us, where there was no chance of him escaping, and even if he tried Ray would flatten him the second he moved — and Ray was a big man. The surprised prisoner, who had no doubt thought he would be locked up in a police cell by that stage, agreed to the arrangement and we spent another half hour enjoying our pints. Ray bought one for his prisoner and the latter even reciprocated and gave me the money to buy us all a final pint before returning to the station, where he was finally charged with burglary.

Most people, especially any serving police officers today, would probably find what Ray and I did that night totally reprehensible. It probably was, however my excuse is that I was only the junior officer. Ray's excuse would be that the prisoner later became one of the best informants he had during his service, and provided him with some excellent arrests.

Our visits to pubs were not frowned upon by our supervising CID officers — far from it, they encouraged it and would often join us for a drink. Excessive drinking was obviously not approved of but this was prior to the introduction of the breathalyser in 1967 and although drivers, including police officers, were aware of the consequences of driving under the influence of drink, they were not concerned or aware of what alcohol limits were legally acceptable or safe. Consequently, I am sure that at that time many of us would have failed a breathalyser test had we been required to take one, something I am not proud of and a sobering thought — pardon the pun.

One well-known detective superintendent I worked under visited a particular pub in south London so frequently that, after he successfully investigated a murder that had occurred near the pub, the landlord had a brass plate put on the wall near the seat he always took when having a drink, which read, "He Solved Them Here". Can you imagine that happening today? I will not name the DS but I learned a great deal from him, he had a reputation as an excellent thief catcher, was very well respected by his junior officers and I am proud to have worked under his experienced guidance.

I respected my informants for the risks they were usually taking and I hoped they respected me enough to divulge good information to me and that I would act upon it accordingly. Respect has to be earned, as does trust; however trust is hard to come by because of the nature of the circumstances and people involved. A police officer would be foolish to trust his informant one hundred per cent.

I had two particularly good informants. The first was a regular customer in a pub I also frequented. I got to know him over a period of time, he was aged about fifty with a wife and children and although he had a number of convictions when he was younger, he had not been to prison for several years. I had the impression that he was jealous of the younger villains he drank with, who were regularly committing crimes and had more money than he did.

He approached me one day and informed that three of his mates were going to break into a tobacconist shop and had offered to pay him as a lookout. They were going to gain entry by climbing a drainpipe at the rear of the premises to the first floor, where cigarettes and tobacco were stored. My informant was unable to climb due to a back injury and his job was to stay on the ground and knock on the drainpipe if he heard anyone approaching.

Being an agent provocateur — i.e. encouraging someone to commit a crime — is an offence in itself, but in this scenario, the police were not setting up the crime but now knew it was going to take place and could take steps to apprehend the perpetrators. I agreed with my informant that we would arrest his mates as they were leaving the building and about to

185

get into their van. He was to walk away from the scene but I would arrest him, my colleagues would arrest the others, and all would be taken to the police station.

The whole operation went like clockwork, myself and four other officers sat in our nondescript police van, watching through the slits cut in the side, as three of the criminal team climbed the drainpipe, smashed a window and gained access, while my informant remained down below. A short time passed and then boxes of cigarettes started to be thrown out of the window, shortly after which the three breakers descended the drainpipe and started to load their van with the booty. As they did so, my informant did not touch the stolen goods but walked round to the front of the premises telling his mates that he was going to check that the coast was clear for them to leave.

On a given signal we jumped out of our vehicle, my colleagues arrested the three loading the van and I went around the corner and arrested my informant, who told me he was "just on his way home from his son's house!" When we arrived back at the station, the three shop breakers couldn't have been more helpful, telling us that "the other man we had arrested had nothing to do with the crime". They didn't even know him, they said. We had not seen him breaking in or helping load the stolen goods and it was very dark, also his son later confirmed his alibi, therefore he was not charged and was released. His criminal compatriots never did find out he was a grass and he received a small reward for his information.

It would be interesting to know how the average member of the public looks upon such a police operation, in fact I don't even know if the police of today would act in the same way in such a scenario. I do know that had my informant not confided in me and I not trusted him, a crime would have been committed and probably never solved. Instead, three active criminals were sent to prison for a while and the public were protected from them.

The pub where I became acquainted with that informant, was a regular watering hole for not only several local criminals but also dockers and local folk who had made it their local over a number of years. I became quite friendly with the landlord and his wife, who eventually emigrated to Australia — in fact I agreed to have their dog when they left.

Another pub I used to visit as a detective on Late Duty was an interesting establishment and also frequented by dock workers. I learned from the landlord that he was also registered as a docker. He rarely went to the docks but was paid a wage. In those days the men worked in gangs of about eight or ten and would sign on every morning and then be allocated to various jobs, mainly loading and unloading ships. The agreement was that one of the gang would sign the pub landlord in for work daily, and come pay day, the pub landlord would keep one week's wages and give the other three weeks' to the rest of his gang — who would quite happily spend it in his pub! I seem to recall that it was his wife who officially held the pub licence but for various reasons I never reported anyone for the scam; perhaps some may think I should have done.

My second informant, I'll call him Ivor, was a well-known local villain, aged about twenty-two, with a number of convictions. I arrested him for possessing drugs, amphetamines, for which he received a short term of imprisonment, and when I next saw him drinking in a local pub he bought me a beer. He told me that since being released from prison he had got married, found a job and was trying to go straight, which he found was difficult as he could not avoid his criminal friends who were constantly trying to get him to help them commit various crimes. He told me that he had given up drugs and desperately wanted to go straight, as his wife was pregnant. One of his associates had some sort of hold over him, I never found out what but suspected that it was to do with money he owed for drugs prior to his last prison term.

Shortly after our meeting in the pub, Ivor phoned me in the CID office and asked to meet. He told me that he had been approached by three of his mates, all of whom had criminal records and were drug addicts. They were going to break into a chemist's to steal drugs and they wanted him to be the car driver. Ivor was particularly scared of one of the three and he also divulged that the gang had broken into two other chemists in the area recently and stolen drugs.

I confirmed that the two break-ins had in fact occurred, and Ivor supplied me with the details of the planned crime and after a couple more clandestine meetings I agreed to him taking part in the offence and that while his cohorts would be arrested when leaving the shop, he would drive off and make his getaway. My supervising detective inspector agreed to the plan and a team of six officers, including myself, was briefed. Everything was in place and at an agreed time Ivor phoned me to confirm that the job was still going ahead, also giving me the registration number and description of the gang's car.

At about midnight, me and the rest of our team set off in two unmarked police cars and parked up about half a mile from the chemist's shop. We were in radio contact with each other via the Scotland Yard network, and as we waited, smoked and chatted in anticipation, I could feel the adrenalin kicking in, as it always did on those sorts of occasions. Ivor had told me that they were going to break in to the premises at 1 a.m., and at about 12.50 a.m. a call came over our car radio which completely changed the outcome of the whole operation! To quote Robert Burns, "The best planned schemes of mice and men . . ."

The call came from one of our uniformed area cars that was in the vicinity and requested we meet them urgently. On arrival at the rendezvous, imagine our amazement when we saw that the crew had stopped the vehicle containing my informant, who was driving, and the other would-be shop breakers. As luck would have it I knew the area car driver, Terry, well and had served with him previously in uniform, but I was astonished when he told me what had transpired. Terry said that he and his crew had stopped the car being driven by

Ivor because only one rear light was working. As the car stopped Ivor had got out immediately, approached Terry, and said, "I need to speak to you without those three in the car hearing. It's OK, Officer, you needn't bother about the car, it's not nicked, it belongs to one of them but I'm insured. We're on our way to bust into a chemist's shop and nick a load of drugs, but your mates know all about it and are waiting, they are going to nick those other three and they're going to let me get away."

"Who are these mates of mine who you say know about it?" Terry asked

"Bob Dixon, do you know him?" Terry confirmed that he did, put Ivor in the police car and then had sent his call on the radio. Together with my colleagues we searched the villains' vehicle, found a crowbar, a torch and a hammer also a small amount of cannabis in the pockets of two of them. In addition, one appeared to be high on drugs of some sort.

All four men were told that they were being arrested for going equipped to steal and two for possession of drugs. When we arrived at the police station the prisoners were interviewed separately and three made statements, not admitting their exact intentions earlier that night but admitted breaking into the chemists that Ivor had told me about earlier. They all stated that Ivor had nothing to do with those offences and in view of the fact that my informant had, on the face of it, committed no offence other than driving with a defective rear light, and knew nothing about the breaking equipment found in the car, he was released without charge. The other three were charged with going equipped to steal and the two breakings. I particularly remember interviewing one of the villains in the CID office, who was obviously high on drugs, because part of my subsequent evidence in court of that interview was, "The defendant then had an incoherent conversation with a cupboard, My Lord," to which the judge, who obviously had a sense of humour, quipped, "I take it the cupboard did not reply, Officer."

All officers, whether uniformed or CID, liked to be recorded on charge sheets as the arresting officer and I insisted that Terry should be shown as such for one of the prisoners. He acted totally professionally and had been so understanding in handling a difficult and unusual situation that few uniformed officers would expect to deal with. The three prisoners were subsequently sent to prison completely unaware that Ivor had "grassed them up". Ivor received no reward but was more than happy that he had finally rid himself of acquaintances with whom he no longer wished to associate.

That story is a classic example of what could go wrong when dealing with informants and luckily it was a comparatively minor offence that ended successfully and resulted in three active criminals being taken off the streets. However, only specialist, highly trained and experienced officers would deal with informants who provide information regarding guns, terrorists, bombs, kidnapping and threats to the public.

Not all informants received rewards, the decisions were made by senior officers and such factors as the value to the public of the information given would be assessed. As a beat constable, it was fairly unusual but not unknown to give a minor criminal just a few pounds for information that led to an arrest and I did that a couple of times. As an aid to CID or as a detective we were able to claim small expenses for drinks purchased in public houses for possible or actual informants.

Informants come in all shapes and sizes and an amusing incident occurred when I was in uniform and, accompanied by another constable, went to a flat where a minor criminal lived. He was wanted and we were in possession of an arrest warrant that had been issued for failing to appear in court to answer to a theft charge. We knocked on the door, which was opened by his wife, with a small boy aged about four years standing behind her. My colleague and I entered the premises and the woman told us that she had not seen her husband for several days, but to our — and her — surprise her son said, "Daddy's in the cupboard in the bedroom."

I went to the cupboard and found the wanted man hiding under a pile of clothing; I always remember him kissing his son on the head and saying, "Never mind, son, you'll learn when you get older." I wonder how long it took for the little lad to understand that "grassing" on your own flesh and blood was not the done thing?

★　★　★

A strange incident happened involving my mother, and I always wondered if it was in some way connected to my using informants, having arrested some local villain.

When my father died, my mother had moved to live quite near us. I was an aid at the time, and I received a phone call from my mother, who sounded very worried. She wanted to confirm that I was OK as she had a phone call from someone purporting to be a shopkeeper, who told her that her police officer son had been seriously injured in a road accident outside his shop and that he had obtained her phone number from "her son's pocket" before he was taken to hospital. I, of course, told her I was perfectly all right and never did get to the bottom of that despicable phone call. My mum did not have an ex-directory phone number at the time but we quickly changed that.

Another rather more amusing incident involving my mother happened when somebody phoned her stating that he was a Detective Sergeant Harris from the local police station. He told her that he had interviewed a man who was suspected of making indecent phone calls but through lack of evidence had been released. However, the DS said that among the suspect's possessions was a list of phone numbers, including my mother's. DS Harris advised my mother that he had arranged for her phone line to be tapped for a few days and if she were to receive any indecent phone calls she should try and keep the caller talking for as long as possible in order that the police could trace the call.

My mother agreed, and a few hours later — surprise, surprise — she received a call. The caller did not take long to "get to the point", asking my mother what colour knickers she was wearing, what size bra she wore, etc. My mum was always quite prudish and, bearing in mind she was over sixty years old and a widow at the time, although embarrassed, she did surprisingly well to keep the caller talking for several minutes. She waited a short while and then rang the local police station to speak to Detective Sergeant Harris. Guess what? There was no DS Harris, he didn't exist! Mother did actually see the funny side of things and accepted my gentle admonishment for not phoning me at the very start of the incident.

I can't leave the subject of informants without giving some small insight into the minds of some criminals, particularly the ones who would describe themselves as "hardened career criminals". These villains would rarely become informants and to my mind they have a different view of life, different values and morals, than the usual man in the street. I got to know several in this category and their views that I am going to describe are what they actually told me, not my interpretation or thoughts on their lifestyles.

As I said earlier, during the time I was in the Met, officers — particularly those in the CID or working in plain clothes — were allowed to enter public houses, clubs, etc., both on and off duty without it being frowned upon or any discipline being taken against them. Because we became quite friendly with certain trustworthy publicans who ran respectable establishments, it was not unusual for us to call in for a drink accompanied by our wives to socialize with regular customers we knew, just as many folk visit their local. I suppose we hoped they would look upon us as part of the community. It was as a result of such visits that I got to know a few career criminals.

Not all villains necessarily frequent what one would call "villains' pubs". Some do of course and those establishments soon gain a reputation, and a copper, even in plain clothes, stands out like a sore thumb. The exception to that was, of course, the Kray brothers who bought and ran their own pubs. However, some career criminals want to give the impression of being an average member of the public and do not go looking for trouble; after all, they are involved in serious crimes that often provide large rewards, the last thing they want is to be arrested for some minor offence like a fight in a pub. Thus it was not unusual for us when socializing in our favourite pubs to see a few of those characters, often with their wives or girlfriends.

Hardened career criminals would rarely commit crimes in the areas in which they lived, they would go much further afield, sometimes many miles or out of London. We police officers were aware that those villains were heavily involved in crime and we knew that they were known to the criminal intelligence branch at Scotland Yard, serious crime squads, such as the flying squad and the regional crime squads all of whom would monitor their movements and target them.

195

These characters were invariably courteous when we saw them in pubs, often acknowledged us and sometimes even had a chat. The interesting thing was that we would occasionally know that they had "done a job". I well remember such an occasion when a colleague and I took our wives out for a meal and a drink to one of our favourite pubs, and among the other customers were three men I knew as career criminals accompanied by three women — two of whom I recognized as their wives. After several minutes, the barman presented us with four glasses of champagne, which he said were with the compliments of the three villains who were sitting at a table further down the bar. I gave them a wave, acknowledging their hospitality, and saw that they had two or three bottles of champagne and were obviously celebrating something. A short while later I went to the Gents' and bumped into one of our benefactors, I'll call him Jeff. I thanked him for the drinks and casually asked what they were celebrating.

"Let's just settle for a birthday, shall we?" he replied. He smiled and winked and I knew it would be imprudent to enquire further.

A few days later I saw Jeff in the same pub, only this time he was on his own. There were just a few regulars drinking and I offered to buy him a pint, which he accepted. I joined him at his table and we started having a general chat about nothing in particular. However, it wasn't long before the subject turned to crime, or more specifically cops and robbers; it turned out to be a fascinating exchange of views.

I knew that Jeff, who was about thirty-five and married with two children, had convictions for armed robbery, lorry hijacking and theft for which he had spent several years in some of Britain's toughest prisons. I indicated that it seemed obvious to me that from the way he had been celebrating on the champagne evening, he and his mates had recently been involved in some sort of lucrative criminal activity. Jeff would not commit himself on that one but said he was fully aware that he was often on the various squads' lists of criminals suspected of serious crimes, some of which he might have been responsible for and others which he was not. He accepted that and said because of the life he and his mates led he just had to try and be one step ahead of the Old Bill.

I asked him if it was not a constant worry to live looking over his shoulder all the time, waiting for a knock on the door, but he said he just accepted it as part of the life he had chosen. His father was a criminal and, like him, he had been one all his life, never having had a job, not claiming benefits for himself or his family and not paying tax.

Jeff then revealingly continued along these lines saying, "Look, mate, you're the mug, not me. You have a family, I guess, that you have to provide for, and so do I. You get up and go to work every day and so do I. I sometimes get up at three, four or five in the morning if we're going to do a hit, so we can set it up properly. It's a serious job to me and important I get it right. If we get it right the perks are usually great, a bloody sight better than yours I bet.

197

"You know I've done a bit of bird in my time and sometimes your lot have stitched me up, which I ain't complaining about. I know you've got a job to do and it's all a bit of a game, some you win and some you lose and that goes for both sides. I know I'll get nicked again sometime and do some more bird but it's worth it. My wife and kids have a good standard of living and when I'm inside I know they will be seen all right and well looked after by my mates, we all have that agreement.

"I've got a great missus. She knew I was a villain when she married me. Her old man was a villain, so she grew up with it and knew what to expect. Look, mate, I'm not making excuses for what I do but I never seriously hurt anyone, I might put the shits up a few people now and again but they can get over it. You've got your steady old job with a pension at the end of it and good luck, but I bet you more dough will go through my hands than it will yours. After all, I could afford to buy a few bottles of bubbly the other night, could you?"

Jeff was possibly right. The Proceeds of Crime Act, which gives the courts the power to confiscate goods and cash obtained as a result of crime, did not come into force until 2002, and no doubt he did benefit from his illegal activities, especially if he was not caught. However, I did not try to impose my views on him. He had revealed some of his morals and lifestyle, which I suppose didn't surprise me greatly. We enjoyed another pint and then went our separate ways. We remained acquaintances for some time and, as he prophesized, he did go back to prison for committing a wages robbery.

Who says crime doesn't pay? Sometimes it definitely does, but at what price?

CHAPTER
TWELVE

Murders

Murders always have been a very interesting part of police work and many Metropolitan Police Officers, both in the uniformed branch and the CID, become part of a murder investigation at some point in their service. During my time, I was involved in four murder investigations, served on three murder squads and was directly involved in the arrests of the perpetrators of three of the crimes.

Murder squads operated somewhat differently back then, mainly due to the incredible advances in technology. In my day we had no computers or CCTV and the investigations, although thorough, were laborious. Generally, a senior officer such as a detective superintendent or detective chief inspector would take charge of the squad, although for cases where an early arrest was likely, a detective inspector might take responsibility.

The squad would use an "actions book" in which was recorded investigation tasks to be carried out. Those actions could include searching premises, interviewing witnesses and suspects, and taking statements accurately, which I enjoyed. A fellow officer

I once worked with had the task of taking a very long witness statement over a period of two days; amazingly, he was able to write with both his right and left hands — and it was impossible to tell where he had switched.

When the action had been carried out the result would be recorded in the actions book and assessed by the senior investigation officer. A very important part of the process was the use of a card index system, which recorded all relevant information gleaned from the actions. On a large murder investigation there could be thousands of cards in the system and hours were spent by deputed officers cross-referencing the information on them. Should some important piece of information inadvertently not be linked, the investigation could be prolonged for hours, days or even weeks. Also, other officers were responsible for the handling, safe keeping and production at court of exhibits in the case.

As I said earlier, the first few hours after a murder are always vitally important to an investigation and very long hours are often worked by the team. I have worked on squads where I didn't get any sleep for up to thirty-six hours or more. It wasn't a matter of not being allowed to go home, just that if the indication was that an early arrest of a murderer was likely and the investigation gathered pace, then the adrenalin would kick in, which kept us all going. I will also confess that on one murder squad I served on, several of us took amphetamine stimulants known as purple hearts, which were popular with youngsters in the club scene in the 1960s and 70s. I don't know where they came from, but they certainly kept one awake for several hours, after which a deep sleep was always welcome.

It was interesting to see the effect on the local population, particularly villains, when a murder took place. I well remember when one murder occurred, a youth had been stabbed, and the instruction from our detective superintendent was to go to local pubs, clubs and cafés and bring in for questioning any local criminals who might have known the deceased. As a result, I think we ended up bringing in about six or eight villains. We locked them up and proceeded to interview them, which took some time — two days in fact. It transpired that none of them were responsible for the killing, however three of them readily admitted to various other crimes they had recently committed in the area. They were happy to admit to burglary, petty theft and receiving stolen property; one even admitted shoplifting from Woolworth's, but the last thing they wanted was to be linked in any way with a murder. Shortly before the last one of those petty criminals was due to be interviewed, the person who had committed the murder was arrested and, naturally, everyone on the squad was delighted and started to relax. As we were celebrating in the CID office with a few drinks — yes, it was like *The Sweeny* at times! — the station sergeant came in and asked the detective superintendent what he wanted to do with the man in the cells. "What man in the cells?"

"The one your lads brought in two days ago," came the reply.

"Oh shit, I thought we'd got rid of that lot. Just apologize, thank him for his patience and kick him out!" That was the last we heard from him.

The first murder case I became involved in occurred when I was in uniform and we were called one night to the Prospect of Whitby public house in Wapping, where the body of a young man had been found outside on the pavement. When we arrived, at about 10.30p.m., CID officers were already there and we were instructed to close the pub, which was very busy, prevent any of the customers from leaving and obtain all their personal details.

The victim was identified as a young university medical student who had been for a night out with his friends and, on leaving the pub, had become involved in a fight with another group of men. The lad had been punched in the face and had fallen backwards, causing him to hit his head on the kerb which, as the post-mortem later showed, fractured his skull. He immediately lost consciousness and died very shortly afterwards at the scene. Within days, the CID arrested his assailant who later pleaded guilty to manslaughter and received a fairly short sentence considering he had killed someone. I felt so sorry for the victim's family who had lost their son at the point when he probably had a great future ahead of him. An example of what can happen as a result of one thoughtless act caused by drink, which doubtless caused so much grief to two families.

★ ★ ★

The murder of a child is always horrific and I was involved in one such case very shortly after becoming an aid to CID. Apart from the importance of trying to detect the murderer, it was my first experience of being attached to a murder squad and gave me a good insight as to how such an operation was directed and carried out by senior officers.

On 1 March 1964, a seven-year-old girl named Kim Roberts who lived in Stepney Way went out to play near her home; she was never seen alive again. Her mum and dad quickly realized something was wrong when Kim failed to come home later that day and immediately reported her missing to Arbour Square Police Station, which was close to the Roberts' home. A full-scale missing person's alert was sent to all stations and the search began. Although Kim was still classed as a missing person, by nightfall there was no trace of her and none of her friends had seen her.

All available officers on H Division, both uniformed and plain clothes, were directed to Arbour Square and under the direction of the detective superintendent were formed into search teams. Word of Kim's disappearance soon spread among the local population and, as one would expect of East Enders, hundreds joined in the hunt. There was extra concern for the girl's safety because it had been an exceptionally cold winter and the temperature was still dropping well below freezing at night. My job was to visit every house in a number of streets in Stepney, collate the details of all occupants, ask if they knew Kim and search any outside buildings and sheds. The teams worked late into the night and commenced again early the next morning, by which time the area was swarming with newspaper and television reporters.

There were no clues as to what had happened to the little girl, she had just vanished and it became clear that we were probably investigating a murder. Unfortunately, our beliefs were sadly well founded. After several days Kim's body was found by a man walking his dog in Epping Forest, her body had been dumped in a ditch about twenty miles from her home. She had been raped and strangled.

At Arbour Square a full murder squad was immediately formed, of which I was part, and shortly after the dreadful discovery, a witness contacted the squad with good information. He stated that shortly before Kim's body was found he was parked in a lay-by close to the location when he saw another car parked on the verge and the driver lifted what appeared to be a large parcel from the boot and walked with it along a track into the forest. The driver returned a short time later, wiping his hands on a piece of rag. The witness asked the man what he was doing and was told to "mind his own business and clear off".

Despite thousands of hours of investigation Kim Roberts' murderer was never found. Thousands of people were interviewed, over 5,700 statements were taken, quite a number by me, but there was no breakthrough. Several suspects were interviewed and released. Senior investigating officers believed very strongly that one local man they questioned was responsible for the crime, but they had insufficient evidence with which to charge him.

After about three months, the murder squad was disbanded except for just a few officers who were left to continue the enquiry. As with any unsolved murder we were disappointed and sad that we had not arrested and convicted anyone, particularly where the evidence points towards a suspect but is insufficient to charge them. It is also devastating for the families and friends of the victim not to have a conviction, especially where a child is involved, as they have to continue grieving without any closure to their tragedy. To this day no one has been charged with Kim Roberts's murder, but the case will always remain open.

As an aid to CID, when on Night Duty, a detective sergeant and two aids would be responsible for covering all police stations on the division. If anyone from the uniform branch arrested somebody for committing a crime (anything classed as a criminal offence, not drunkenness or abusive behaviour), then we would be called to the particular station, hear the evidence and advise the station officer as to whether to charge the prisoner and, if so, with what offence. Obviously, most station officers were experienced and knew as much, if not more, than we did about criminal offences but they sometimes needed guidance with difficult cases and needed advice from our detective sergeant. We would take the fingerprints and personal history of the prisoner, also witness statements and prepare the paperwork ready for the CID the following morning.

206

Our tour of duty was from 10p.m. until about 6a.m. but often longer. Sometimes, when everything on the division seemed quiet, at about 5a.m. the DS and two aids would take it in turns to finish duty and go home. One night that practice nearly backfired on us and I remember it very well.

It was a very cold night in January 1965 and my colleague George and I were on duty with our detective sergeant. We had had a fairly quiet night, and at about 5.45 the DS was not feeling too well so decided to go home, a journey of around ten miles. He was happy that George and I could cope but left instructions that we should phone and inform him of anything he should know about.

Shortly after he had left, George and I were called to Arbour Square Police Station to see a woman who was in a very distressed state. She told us that she was the wife of a man known as Ginger Marks, who was a well-known criminal and well-connected to the Kray twins. Mrs Marks explained that she had received an anonymous telephone call telling her that her husband had been shot dead in Cheshire Street, Bethnal Green. She said that Ginger had gone out earlier that evening for a drink and had said he would be back later. George and I phoned all the local hospitals and ascertained that he had not been admitted, nor had there been any road accidents reported on H Division. Without implying too much to Mrs Marks, we suggested the possibility that her husband might have gone to a party or to stay the night at a friend's house, however she rejected that explanation, saying he would have phoned her.

We instructed the distraught lady to remain at the station, while we went to Cheshire Street. It was still quite dark and the street lights were on as George and I drove up and down Cheshire Street several times and found nothing suspicious. We returned to Arbour Square and informed Mrs Marks of the negative search. We then drove her home, which was nearby and instructed her stay by her phone and if she heard nothing to return to Arbour Square at about 9 a.m. George and I went back to the station, phoned our DS to inform him of what had transpired since he'd gone home and wrote our report for the Day Duty CID.

We were about to go off duty when Mrs Marks came running into the police station crying and screaming. She was accompanied by a man, who was a relative. They explained that they had driven up to Cheshire Street and, on a wall next to a public house, the Carpenter's Arms, they had found a bullet hole and blood on the ground. George and I immediately returned to Cheshire Street and, using our torches, identified the bullet hole, blood and a small amount of body tissue, which was later identified as stomach lining. George remained at the scene and I returned to Arbour Square, where the station sergeant dispatched the Early Turn beat officers who had just come on duty to secure the crime scene.

I telephoned our DS who immediately returned, no doubt breaking the speed limit all the way, but he did arrive before the detective superintendent, who had been roused from his bed. Mrs Marks was looked after at the station and I did not see her again. I made my statement as to the events that night and completed my three weeks of Night Duty but was not part of the murder squad.

The outcome of these events was that Ginger Marks had been shot dead in a gangland killing but his body was never recovered. A notorious criminal named Freddie Foreman, whose son Jamie is today a well-known actor who appears in the television series *EastEnders*, was eventually charged with the murder, tried and acquitted. However, several years later he admitted the murder but was not able to be charged because of the Double Jeopardy Law, since repealed. Foreman was known as an enforcer for the Kray brothers and although the Krays were never implicated in the killing of Ginger Marks, it is interesting to note that the public house, the Carpenter's Arms, was allegedly purchased by the twins for their mother, Violet Kray, who often worked in the pub. It was a well-known meeting place for the brothers, their henchmen and show business characters in the 1960s and even Judy Garland was said to have sung there on more than one occasion. Ginger Marks knew the Krays well and one wonders if he was lured there on the night he disappeared? A great deal has been written about the murder of Ginger Marks but my colleague George and I were the first officers on the scene.

Another murder investigation I was involved in as an aid to CID occurred not far from Leman Street Police

Station one night at about 1 a.m., when a man walked into the station and said he had found the body of a woman in a nearby derelict prefab. He added that he had gone into the building to urinate and stumbled over the body. As a result, the detective sergeant, my colleague and I took the man back to the location.

The prefab was one of several in a street, which had been built just after the war to house the East Enders whose homes had been bombed. They were all completely derelict, there were no other buildings, and the area was quite dark. The man led us around the back of two prefabs, well back from the road, and into a third. There, in the light from our torches, lying on the floorboards, was the body. She had obviously been badly beaten, mutilated and sexually abused. The sight was horrific, one of the most dreadful I witnessed during my police service. We immediately used the CID car radio to request uniformed assistance in order to seal off the crime scene and to await the scenes of crime officer. We returned to the police station with the man, to take his witness statement and to phone senior officers.

My colleague and I agreed with the DS that the scenario we had been presented with just did not add up. The man who had allegedly discovered the body was dirty, unkempt and, at best could be described as a vagrant; he said he had no fixed address and lived in hostels. Why would such a character bother to go to such a remote and isolated spot to urinate when there was no likelihood of anyone seeing him; why not go to the first prefab, instead of walking in the dark to the third? He was definitely a suspect. When we started to question the man and put these anomalies to him he immediately admitted that he had killed the woman. He was officially cautioned and told that he was being arrested on suspicion of murder.

Enquiries revealed that the dead woman was a local prostitute who was aged about fifty and had four children. She had solicited the man and taken him to the prefab but it transpired he had no money. This caused an argument, which culminated in her brutal murder, although why he had to abuse the poor woman's body in the way he did I'll never know. He eventually appeared at the Old Bailey, pleaded guilty to the murder and was sentenced to life imprisonment. Meanwhile the victim's children were put into local authority care.

Old people who live alone are always very vulnerable — and easy targets for those inclined to take advantage of them, in whatever way. Such old folk are often lonely and welcome friendship from anyone who helps them or shows an interest in them. There were many such old ladies who lived in the East End, several having been widowed as a result of the Second World War and one of them, Grace, resided alone in Bow. She was well liked by all her neighbours, some of whom often did her shopping and helped her in any way they could.

The old lady was about eighty years old and, although very crippled with arthritis, went out for short walks when she felt up to it. On most fine days she would sit in a chair on the pavement outside her house, and in common with many cockney ladies of her age she was very proud of her immaculately clean red-brick step and polished brass door knocker. Grace would pass the time of day with anyone, whether she knew them or not, and she was well known for chatting to the local children, often letting them enter her house. Several would call on Grace after school and ask if she wanted any errands doing; even if she didn't she would sometimes give them a few pence to go and buy some sweets at the corner shop.

One day in the summer of 1966, neighbours became concerned about Grace as she had not been seen for two days and her two pints of milk were still on the doorstep, so they called the police. A constable from Bow Police Station went to the house and, on getting no reply to his knocking, broke a window at the rear of the premises with his truncheon and climbed in. On going into Grace's living room he was confronted with a horrific sight: she was sitting in her chair, fully clothed, but clearly dead. Immediately it was obvious Grace had not died from natural causes because her hands were tied and she had very severe injuries to her head. The local CID was called, a murder squad formed and the investigation commenced.

The enquiries continued and at the time I was an aid to CID, again performing Night Duty throughout H Division with a colleague and a detective sergeant. We, of course, knew of Grace's murder and there was a rumour, which was never confirmed, that the Kray twins had offered an unofficial reward for the arrest of the murderer (their mother, Violet, lived nearby).

One night, things were fairly quiet and so we decided to cruise around the division in the CID car. At about 12.30 a.m., I can't remember exactly where we were, but we noticed two very young youths walking along the street. Realizing it was far too late for boys that young to be out, we decided to stop them. They said that they were on their way home from a friend's house, however when we searched them their pockets were full up with packets of cigarettes and sweets. We quickly ascertained on the car radio that a local newsagent's shop had been broken into and we took the boys back to the police station. It turned out that they were brothers, aged fourteen and twelve. They were put in separate detention rooms to await the arrival of their parents, but while waiting, the detective sergeant and I sat with the youngest boy and he made an astonishing admission.

Without being questioned or put under any pressure whatsoever, he started to cry and said, "It wasn't my fault, my brother made me do it, he wanted the fags, not me." He then went on to say that he was always taking the blame for what his brother did and that they hadn't meant to kill the old lady, just to frighten her to get her money. On asking him exactly what he was talking about, he admitted that he and his brother had beaten Grace to death. During my police career I gradually learned that nothing much surprised me, however I was shocked at this young lad's sudden revelation. The boy was told that he was being arrested on suspicion of murder and officially cautioned. We immediately contacted the murder squad who were still working twenty-four hours a day and informed them that we had apprehended their murderers.

It transpired at the boys' trial that they had known Grace well and often visited her at home, pretending to be her friend but sometimes stealing her money. They both had criminal records, despite their ages, and pleaded guilty to murder, for which they were detained at Her Majesty's Pleasure — meaning they would not be released until the authorities felt it safe to do so. What a sad way for an old lady's life to come to an end, and what a way for two young boys to ruin their futures when so young and with their lives ahead of them. I wonder what made them commit such a brutal crime — can a child be just plain evil?

The final murder I will briefly describe occurred in Woolwich, South London, when I was a detective constable. A man aged about twenty-five was involved in a fight with a youth on a railway bridge late on a Friday night, which resulted in him being stabbed to death. It was very quickly established that the murderer was a particularly vicious well-known local thug. The next day, soldiers from the local barracks were called in to help the police search the railway embankment and area for the murder weapon, but it wasn't found. Later that day we received an anonymous call informing us that the suspect was in a local fish and chip shop and, in view of the fact that I had arrested him previously for a serious assault and could therefore recognize him, a detective sergeant and I were instructed to go and arrest him. We went to the fish and chip shop, grabbed both his arms and told him we were arresting him on suspicion of murder; he did not resist.

At the station, the youth was charged with the murder and detained in a cell awaiting his appearance at court the next day. Later that evening, his girlfriend appeared, demanding to know why her boyfriend had been detained and wanting to see him. This was refused, whereupon she became extremely abusive and violent and was arrested. She was searched by a woman police officer and a knife was found hidden in her bra. The knife was subsequently scientifically examined and proved to be the murder weapon used by the youth.

An interesting footnote to that story was that when the youth's file arrived from the Scotland Yard criminal records office it not only listed his previous convictions, of which there were many, mainly for vicious assaults, but a note had been recorded a few years earlier by a detective who had dealt with him that read, "This man is dangerous and will probably commit murder one day." Prophetic words indeed.

CHAPTER
THIRTEEN

On Reflection

My dear old mother-in-law used to frequently tell me, "Life was so much better in the old days, we had everything we wanted and didn't have to rely on modern technology."

In reply to that I'd say, "Yes, it must have been great, after all, you had diphtheria, polio, whooping cough, outside toilets, and the kids were shoved up chimneys!"

My point was that every generation seems to think that life was so much better in bygone eras and if one was lucky enough, as I was, to have had a great childhood, memories tend to consist of looking back on long hot summers without a care in the world. But of course it is a mistake to view history through rose-tinted glasses.

Nevertheless, I also think that there is a great deal of value in the cliché, "If it ain't broke, don't fix it". I am all for advancing modern technology, science and thinking where they improve our lives, however there must surely be certain aspects of our lives that should not be changed just for the sake of it and any changes that are made should incorporate proven methods that work.

My wife puts it rather succinctly when she points out that despite changes in the medical profession, involving great advancements in medicine and surgery, some practices that took place up to fifty years ago and even longer when she started her nursing training are still used in, or are being revived by, hospitals today — for example the use of poultices, leeches and maggots! It is possible to combine the past with the present.

So how does this relate to the Metropolitan Police Force? Well, I believe some things that I saw and did in the 1960s and 70s could be incorporated into today's modern police forces. It will come as no surprise to know that the one thing I feel most strongly about is the bobby on the beat, and I firmly believe that the general public would benefit so much from seeing a copper walking the streets in their local communities again.

I have attempted to describe what life was like for a policeman performing his duties in the East End of London fifty years ago, and no doubt some may find how we dealt with certain situations abhorrent or unprofessional; others may think them funny, understandable and acceptable. I am not going to either defend or excuse anything, I am ashamed of nothing I did during my police service and every decision I made or action I took was done with the best of intentions. Possibly, on occasions, I might have done things differently, but of course hindsight is a wonderful thing. I simply ask the reader to try and have an open mind when judging the actions of myself and my colleagues and relate them to the era in which we were working, and not to compare them with what we see from our police today. I hope, however, that like me you might think the modern day police service could learn a thing or two from the experience of officers who served the public in the past.

A subject about which the modern police are particularly sensitive is gratuities. There is a huge difference between a gratuity, which can best be described as something given by way of thanks without any obligation or expectation, and a bribe, which is something given, often illegally, with the hope or expectation of receiving a gain or influence in return. Bearing that in mind, the reader might like to reflect on some of the incidents I have described in earlier chapters while patrolling the Limehouse beats and others I will describe.

During our training at Peel House the subject of accepting bribes was mooted by one of our instructors. He told us to assume we were going to serve for thirty years, work out approximately what our total salary would be for that period, allowing for increases, assume we would live for a further twenty years in retirement receiving a pension, allow for inflation over the whole period, and then calculate the total. He said if we were offered a bribe that was above that total it was probably worth accepting it, if not we should tell the person making it to "get stuffed".

When I was in uniform it was never required for me to report to any senior officer the fact that I had entered a premises and been given a cup of tea or accepted a bag of biscuits. A bobby on his beat calling in for cup of tea from time to time was a great way of getting to know local residents, shopkeepers and business people, and to keep abreast with what was happening in the community.

There were some favours that would definitely not be acceptable today. When I was a CID officer in 1966 I investigated a factory breaking and theft that took place on Leman Street's ground. I subsequently arrested and charged two men with the breaking and a third for receiving stolen goods, expensive women's clothing. The factory owner was particularly pleased with the outcome because, not only had he recovered most of his stolen goods, but one of the criminals was a man who worked for him.

The owner had strong connections with West Ham Football Club and the World Cup was about to take place in England. Being a bit of a football fanatic, I was delighted when, by way of thanks, the factory owner gave me two tickets for the opening ceremony, which included England's opening game of the tournament against Uruguay. Pretty well everyone at Leman Street got to hear of my good fortune and absolutely nobody, senior officers included, intimated in any way that I had accepted a bribe.

I also arrested and prosecuted a local villain for breaking into a fashion shop and stealing several fairly expensive dresses. As a thank you, the lady who owned the shop gave me a catalogue and told me to tell my wife to select two dresses, which she did. I was only doing my job but the shop owner insisted on showing her appreciation. Was that a bribe? Definitely not. But it would not be acceptable today.

In previous chapters I have described a number of incidents involving both myself and other officers entering public houses and drinking when on duty and also socially, but I hope I have not given the impression that, especially in the CID, our time was just spent drinking — far from it. In the 1960s the reason that it was not frowned upon or as strictly controlled as it is with the officers of today was because it was blindingly obvious that criminals frequented pubs and clubs, as they still do. In general, honest hard-working men frequent the greasy spoon café, talk about football and put the world to rights, as do some petty villains, however, hardened career criminals are more likely to meet and converse in more salubrious surroundings and spend their ill-gotten gains.

It was not unknown for publicans, restaurant owners and the like to request that their local beat bobby visited their premises briefly on certain evenings, especially weekends when trouble could occur. By just calling in to ask if everything was OK and be seen by the customers hopefully a message was sent to would-be troublemakers that the police were patrolling the area. I recall doing just that when in plain clothes and visiting a Wimpy Bar, which often attracted unruly youths — McDonald's, hadn't arrived in the UK in those days — and the owner welcomed us. Not only did it help him to run a successful business, as on a couple of occasions we helped him eject troublemakers, but also we became acquainted with the local hooligans and they with us.

While there, we would have a coffee and sometimes a burger for which we would always offer to pay — and often did — but at other times the owner insisted that our refreshments were on the house. The same applied when we visited pubs, we would often buy the landlord or his bar staff a drink and at other times he or she would reciprocate. When in plain clothes and entering licensed premises we did record the fact in our daily diaries but we certainly did not have to seek permission to enter. We only recorded the names of people we met there if we were officially claiming expenses for buying them refreshments.

How times have changed though. A recent article in the *Mail on Sunday* reported that "Paranoid police have something to declare: a sandwich and orange juice". It stated that police today feel under pressure to declare every box of chocolates or bottle of wine given to them because they are fearful of being disciplined, or even arrested. The article gave the example that one member of the Met declared a single cup of tea while another declared a sandwich and a bottle of orange juice given to him during a visit to a supermarket. A Met Police Federation representative said that hospitality should be declared, and as officers were being disciplined for very minor offences they can't afford to fall foul of the rules and even accepting a box of chocolates could cost the recipient his job. I guess the following behaviour would be out of the question today then . . .

Christmas is always a time for most of us to enjoy ourselves and often to thank those who have helped or assisted us in some way during the year. When I was a police officer we celebrated like everybody else. Although each Met district had their sports and social clubs, Christmas celebrations tended to be kept far more local, and took place either at police stations or locations nearby, usually function rooms in public houses. It was quite usual in those days for many police stations outside the Met to have their own social clubs, all selling alcohol on the premises. I visited several, including Southend, Brighton and Worthing, but I understand that is not generally the case today, many have been shut. The only place I knew of such an arrangement in the Met was the police club at Scotland Yard, which was known as the Tank and where I did down a pint or two on infrequent visits.

When in uniform, I enjoyed several Christmas parties that were held in the adjacent section house and, as with the CID parties, it was always the custom to invite members of the local community — publicans, shopkeepers, restaurateurs and business people. We would all contribute towards the cost of the food and some drink, but as with any invited party guest, most would donate bottles of wine and spirits and, at Limehouse, the Chinese and Indian restaurant owners always arrived with dishes of their wonderful spicy food.

The CID parties were similar, but at most of the stations where I served we held them in the office. We would first cover up any official or sensitive information that was displayed on the notice boards. Most of the local publicans, who for some reason we referred to as "Cocks", looked forward to the gatherings and invariably donated large amounts of alcohol. Those parties were attended not only by the local officers but also by senior officers from the division and invited officers from other CID offices. It was always a race to have the first Christmas party; some were held very early in December in order that we would be free to accept the many invitations to other parties that would come in, and all those festivities were held with the full authority and knowledge of our senior officers. I only ever attended one at which an unsavoury incident occurred, which resulted in an officer being transferred, and that was in a county force, not the Met.

One particular person we had a lot of dealings with, both in uniform and the CID, was a scrap metal dealer who also owned a pig farm. Although metal dealers do not always have the best of reputations, we found him to be honest and he kept his business records scrupulously in order for our inspection. At Christmas, he would phone our office and ask for one of us to go to his yard and pick up a Christmas gift. We would go there and our benefactor would load a whole pig carcass into the boot of our car. We then took it to the local hospital mortuary, where the mortician would cut up the pig into joints, keeping one for himself. The rest were shared out between the officers — and we subsequently enjoyed the most succulent pork joints for Christmas.

An amusing activity that I took part in was the Glee Club, which was made up of five police officers, two from the uniformed branch and three from the CID. We all played various instruments including piano, guitar, banjo, drums and I played the spoons — an art my father taught me at an early age. We would meet about once a month on a Sunday lunchtime, when off duty, at a local pub, which was patronized very much by local cockney folk. There was a regular pianist who banged out the usual sing-along tunes and at some time during the proceedings "The Coppers' Glee Club", as the locals called us, would be asked to do a turn. I can't remember how the whole thing started or how our hidden talents were discovered but I do recall all the regular customers in the pub loving it and joining in as we gave them our rendition of "Roll Out the Barrel" and "Maybe It's Because I'm a Londoner". On quite a few occasions a well-known detective superintendent would join us — his speciality was doing a sand dance as per music hall act Wilson, Keppel and Betty, and he also recited amusing poetry and prose. The pub landlord loved us going to his hostelry as it was good for business and he would lay on cheese and biscuits, pickled onions, shellfish and jellied eels for everyone.

Those Sunday lunchtime gatherings were yet another way for us, the police, to get to know some of our locals and for them to get to know us. Surely that was good public relations, but I wonder if it would be allowed today.

To me it seems illogical and sad that today's police should not be allowed to accept any small gifts

224

whatsoever as thank yous for a job well done. It can only help generate good will with the locals. I am fully aware of the dangers of generally allowing gratuities to be accepted but surely common sense and strict rules should be used.

It is hard, really, to try to compare police practices during my years of service with those of today, society and everyday life have changed beyond all recognition. We now live in a world of global crime, where, with the use of computer technology, it's possible for anyone anywhere in the world to steal the identity of another person, or steal vast amounts of money from banks and businesses. Also, terrorist atrocities can be activated simply by pressing a button on a mobile phone.

Some of the most prevalent crimes in the 1960s and 70s were hijacking and stealing lorries and their valuable cargos, protection rackets, long-firm frauds and bank robberies. As a result of the advancement of modern security systems those crimes have diminished greatly. The most recent figures show that the average amount stolen in a bank robbery is only around £30,000, so with, say, four or five villains carrying out a bank raid, they would only benefit by about £6,000 each; hardly worth the risk. The consequence of this is that today's criminals are far more involved in drug-related crimes and computer frauds and it is hardly surprising that their modus operandi have become more sophisticated.

★ ★ ★

When I patrolled the streets of East London I was given a truncheon, a whistle and a torch. Today an officer will have a radio, a baton, handcuffs and a stab-proof vest — some have Tasers and pepper spray. They will have the quick back-up of armed units, riot squads and helicopter cover, if required. Of course, there will be occasions when all those things are necessary for the police but it has been mooted by some that today's patrolling officers look intimidating, even threatening. It is quite rare to see them wearing the distinctive helmet, which in my day represented not only authority and respect but also friendliness.

I grew up in a small village and the local bobby lived there in a police house. Everyone in the community knew him and he knew most of them, he was on call twenty-four hours a day and patrolled on foot or on his cycle, not in a car. As a child, I was brought up to respect him and fear him in a small way; I knew he would give me a telling off if he saw me riding my bike without lights. However, above all I was taught that the local village bobby was a friend who would help people who needed it. He was truly a real life "George Dixon" and every community had one. Happily, a few of those characters can still be found today in rural communities, but far too few.

The outcome of this, sadly in my opinion, is that the "bread and butter" crimes, which are still carried out by petty, spur-of-the-moment criminals, appear to be way down the list of police investigation and importance. A house burglary for any victim, let alone an old person living alone, is as important and frightening to them as a major crime to anyone else. I sometimes wonder if the way some modern day police forces deal with minor crimes is as a result of little consideration for public relations, lack of resources, budgetary constrictions — or a mixture of all three.

I dealt with several house burglaries, both as a uniformed and CID officer. To be a victim of such a crime is very traumatic, especially if the offender has broken in while the householder is on the premises, say, during the night or if the criminal has, as some do, completely ransacked the property and even defecated on the carpets. In my experience it was often fairly easy to evaluate the possibility of arresting a perpetrator of such a crime at an early stage. However, despite the fact that I might consider a quick arrest unlikely, I would give the crime my full attention and, more importantly, show the victim I was doing so. Of course an officer has to be alert to the possibility that the scenario has been created by the householder in order to make a false insurance claim. That was usually easy to detect. A "genuine" burglar would generally leave signs — he is usually in a hurry to carry out the crime and when searching for items to steal from a chest-of-drawers, for example, will start by opening the bottom drawer first, not bother to close it, and then work his way up through the other drawers. A fake burglary might be indicated by all drawers being opened only slightly or all closed. Also, I was suspicious when an alleged victim told me exactly what items had been stolen at my first visit; sometimes it can take several weeks for a victim to discover exactly what has been taken.

As a beat officer and first on the scene I would always look for any obvious clues such as prominent fingerprints and footprints and, if none were evident, I would ask the victim to touch nothing until a detective had attended. I would then talk to neighbours and glean any information I could, prior to returning to or phoning the station, requesting the attendance of a CID officer. When a detective, I visited the premises as soon as possible, dusted for fingerprints and searched for any other clues. If I found good prints I would phone and ask for a SOCO to attend, who would dust for fingerprints again, photograph them and "lift" them with sticky tape in order to preserve them for possible use as evidence in court. As a CID officer I would also make house-to-house enquiries in the locality. A record was kept at the station of all actions that had been taken and two or three days later, as investigating officer, I would revisit the premises.

The important thing about all this was that not only was it vital to be thorough with the investigation of the crime, but the victim could see that something was being done. On many occasions, when a criminal was arrested for an offence he or she would admit others they had committed in order to wipe the slate clean, as they knew only too well that they could be charged with any of those offences if fingerprints showed that they were responsible and receive additional punishment. Those offences were known as Taken Into Consideration (TIC) and it was always a pleasure to visit a burglary victim, often months after the offence was committed, and inform them that we had arrested the culprit, sometimes, if we were lucky, even recovering and returning some of the stolen property.

I have been unlucky enough to recently be the victim of a burglary and it was interesting to witness the methods used by the police today when I reported the crime. My comments are not meant to be a criticism of the methods used today, just a comparison with when I was in the force. My wife and I were away on holiday when the offence took place and my daughter was looking after the house. A uniformed officer did attend, but no search or dusting for fingerprints took place, no SOCO attended, no enquiries were made locally and, interestingly, no police officer visited me on my return. I was just phoned and asked to supply them with a list of stolen property, none of which was ever recovered. I was sent a brochure on advice about securing my home and the phone number of a victim support group.

That experience, to me, indicates the downgrading of the importance of burglary investigation for whatever reason and I could give two other examples of people much older than me being victims of crime and receiving very little or no support from the police.

I do wonder where we're going when I see in a recent newspaper article that several police forces, including the Met, on deciding there is no chance of apprehending and prosecuting a perpetrator of a burglary or mugging are sending out letters to the victims involved stating so, and to placate the victims they are sent a bunch of flowers! That's all well and good but I think that one such victim summed it up when she said she would have rather been visited by a police officer and given some support. It wouldn't take much time for a bobby to call round, tell the lady that there was not a great deal of hope of immediately catching her burglar but he and his colleagues were still looking, and will be keeping a particular eye open around the area for anyone acting suspiciously. Those few words would have a more lasting effect on the victim than a bunch of flowers, wouldn't they? But of course this assumes that the manpower is available to do so.

The three things that seem to hamper today's police are budgets, paperwork and political correctness. During my time there were obviously budgets that senior officers had to control but it was a word we, as beat officers, rarely heard; if it was necessary to work overtime, we did so and got paid for it. Today's police budgets appear to be totally inadequate, although recently funds have been found to appoint and pay for "police tsars".

There was a fair amount of paperwork to be completed, especially when making an arrest that involved taking witness statements and preparing a case for court. However, generally, the beat officer would not be taken off the street for long periods to be able to complete numerous forms relating to minor incidents he had dealt with, which seems to be the practice today.

This has possibly been brought about by the new obsession with taking legal action over anything and everything and the public's awareness of actions or behaviour that might fall into the category of not being "politically correct" — an expression I never heard in Limehouse in the 1960s. The police officers of today are undoubtedly very aware of the possibility of complaints against them resulting in large compensation payments, some of which may be justified. However, when one hears of serving officers suing their employers for what appears to be a frivolous reason one wonders what message that gives to their colleagues and the public.

In 1931, Prime Minister Ramsay Macdonald appointed Hugh Trenchard Commissioner of the Metropolitan Police and he served in that office until 1935. During his tenure, Trenchard made two decisions which greatly changed the structure of the Met. First, he founded the Police Training Centre at Hendon, renamed the Peel Centre when rebuilt in 1974; and second, he introduced The Trenchard Scheme, which was designed specifically for bright school leavers and university students to undertake selected training, join the Met at junior officer level and attain accelerated promotion. The scheme was akin to military procedures. It was not welcomed by the rank and file of the serving officers, and following Trenchard's retirement in 1935 it was scrapped, the lesson having been learned that the making of a good police officer was founded on his experience of patrolling a beat.

That criterion has lasted up until today, although recently it has been mooted that a similar scheme to Trenchard's might be tried. I hope not as I am firmly

231

convinced that even in today's world there can be no replacement for the experience gained from beat patrols. Back in the 1960s, regardless of one's educational qualifications or aspirations we had to spend a minimum of two years patrolling the streets as a constable; there was no accelerated promotion or automatic entry via university.

In 2002 the Metropolitan Police introduced Police Community Support Officers (PCSOs). They are civilian members of police staff appointed as uniformed, non-warranted officers; there are now approximately 16,000 employed in forces across England and Wales and the training varies from force to force. In the Met, it was originally for three weeks, which was considered inadequate and so later increased to six. In other forces it varies between four and eleven weeks, and ongoing training is also carried out. As a result, many foot patrol police officers have been put in cars. Apart from a few exceptions, PCSOs do not have any more powers than you or me, they generally do not have the powers of arrest because they are not attested constables under Section 24 of the Criminal Evidence Act of 1984. They can make a citizen's arrest and no doubt many do a good job. However, now we are in a strange situation: PCSO is a full-time appointment giving a salary of between £16,000 and £27,000 per annum but with very limited powers of arrest, whereas a special constable is a part-time, voluntary appointment with no salary (although some forces do pay expenses), and they have the full powers of arrest of a police officer.

The specials can trace their origins back to the early 1800s and the act passed then still forms the basis of the constitution of today's special constabulary. During my service I worked with some very good and dedicated male and female specials, but sadly today their numbers seem to be diminishing; it's easy to see why.

When I underwent my training at Peel House I was instructed that it was not possible to verbally abuse a police officer unless another member of the public was present and likely to be offended, in which case the abuser could be arrested for behaviour likely to cause a breach of the peace, under the Vagrancy Act of 1824. If a person was shouting and swearing in the street there would invariably be other people in the vicinity and the offender was arrested, but I can't recall ever being abused or sworn at when patrolling by any of the Limehouse yobs; if they had they would have been dealt with. I wonder if respect, no matter how little, had anything to do with it, even fifty years ago.

The 1824 Vagrancy Act is still applicable, although much of it has been amended by subsequent legislation. However, under Section 4 of the Public Order Act a person can still be arrested for threatening, abusive or insulting words and behaviour. With that in mind, why today do I sometimes despair when in my home town, as in many others across the country, on a Friday and Saturday night I see hoards of drunken youths roaming the streets using foul language and having no regard whatsoever for the onlooking police officers, who seem powerless, for whatever reason, to do anything? I suppose it's a reflection of our society — but might I suggest a solution? Why not have a "zero tolerance" approach and carry out a complete purge on street drunkenness for several weeks. Some of those youngsters who get blind drunk and become abusive no doubt come from respectable families and have regular jobs. If they were arrested, their names would be in the local paper and they would be absent from work in order to attend court. Fines might be imposed for a first offence followed by community service.

All too simple, I suppose, and, of course, I suspect budgets would prevent anything like that happening. The other factor when considering a solution is something the police can't have any influence on, the ridiculously cheap alcohol sold by the supermarkets. During my time in East London I dealt with numerous drunks but they were adults, I don't ever remember arresting anyone under the legal age to consume alcohol for being drunk. Obviously, underage drinking did occur but the local population did not suffer from the effects of it.

I am not against change, and there are many things that assist the police of today in their fight against crime, probably the most important being the advancement of forensic science. The use of DNA in crime detection has been invaluable to them but of course it has also been to the advantage of defendants in a number of cases, some where innocent people have served long terms of imprisonment. For example, Stefan Kiszko was convicted of a child killing in 1976 and served sixteen terrible years in prison until in 1992, when DNA proved him innocent of the crime and Ronald Castree guilty.

There are other cases where DNA and modern scientific findings have produced doubt as to the safety of convictions and possible miscarriages of justice involving persons who were hanged, for example, Timothy Evans in the Christie case and James Hanratty for the A6 murder.

In addition to DNA, other areas of forensic science that can assist both prosecution and defence are examination of drugs, chemical testing of police notebooks, statements and video recordings, all of which are important to show that justice is not only done, but seen to be done.

One other thing that has changed is that the villains of today are far more knowledgeable and made aware of their rights. In the 1960s it was not that common for an accused person, even after being cautioned, to reply "no comment" to every question. Obviously, some experienced criminals would not say anything until advised by their solicitor, indeed I remember arresting one who immediately produced a card from his wallet that had his solicitor's phone number on and the words, "In the event of my client's arrest please telephone this number immediately — he will say nothing until he has been advised by me".

We did not use tape recordings or videos of interviews as is the practice today and, of course, an accused person does not and should not have to say anything when questioned. However, understandably, it seems strange to some people that today a person who is totally innocent of a crime should say nothing when given the opportunity to do so in order to prove their innocence. My view on that is No Comment!

Capital punishment was abolished in this country in 1965 and I am often asked if I believe that it should be reintroduced. My answer is that I'm not sure, which I suppose is a cop out (pardon the pun). In 1955, at the age of fourteen, I spoke in a school debate on the subject and proposed that hanging should be abolished. My reasoning was based on the famous case of Christopher Craig and Derek Bentley in 1952, when Bentley was hanged for the fatal shooting of a police constable; Craig was not hanged as he was only sixteen at the time of the murder. The highly controversial point about the case was that Craig fired the gun that killed the constable, whereas Bentley was in police custody at the time and allegedly shouted, "Let him have it, Chris." According to law he was an accomplice and hanged. Even at the young age of fourteen I felt that was unjust and did so for many years.

During my time in the police I still held that view but remember very few colleagues who agreed with me about the death penalty and I admit I did agree with it when I heard of child murders or with the killing of the police officers in West London in 1966.

The conclusion I have come to is that we should consider the system as in most American states whereby homicide is categorized by degree, i.e. first, second and third degree murder, depending on the nature and circumstances of the crime, and set the punishments, including the death penalty, accordingly. I know of at least two very well-known QCs who agree with this and I am sure there are others. The one thing I have learned from my police experience is not to prejudge situations and — especially when considering the question of capital punishment — one should not reach a conclusion based on emotion, which is not always that easy.

I left the met many years ago and am only qualified to criticize today's policing methods from the point of view of a lay person. I will leave it to the reader to have their own views on my method of policing and what they see now. What does sadden me is that the public today do not seem to have as much faith and respect in the police as our public did for us fifty years ago.

I've tried to paint a true picture of what life was like for a London copper in the 1960s and conveyed the pride I have in being lucky enough to have worn the uniform of a bobby on the beat. Would I recommend a child of mine to join the police service today? "No comment!"

Also, a few words of advice for any kind hearted little old ladies who today might think about taking bags of apples or other goodies to the lads at the nick. Don't bother, because a) they might be looked upon as unacceptable gratuities, b) you might find your local police station is no longer there and c), even if it is there, depending on the time of day you visit it might be closed. All three of those possibilities certainly apply in several areas that I am familiar with, but perhaps I should not identify them . . .

Epilogue

Returning to Limehouse

When I was writing this book, I kept wondering how my old stamping ground has changed since I was there over fifty years ago. At first the thought of nostalgic memories being dashed gave me reservations about going back. However, having nearly completed my writing, I decided to make that trip back in time — and having done so I find it a little difficult to put some of my feelings into words.

The first thing that shocked me, although I must have been fairly naive to think it wouldn't, was the complete and utter change in the East End and the area around Limehouse. Several of the police stations have gone and been replaced by rows of shops, but I was pleased to find Limehouse nick still there and looking, from the front in West India Dock Road at least, more or less the same as when I was there. I went into the station and spoke to a couple of officers who were most helpful, describing briefly their present-day duties, although for obvious security reasons they did not go into detail or allow me to look round the building. The public front entrance has changed somewhat, as in all police stations today, in that there is a waiting area for the public and only one person at a time is allowed to go to the front counter. While I was waiting to be seen, I thought it quite amusing that among the five or six other people waiting were a couple who had evidently been there for quite some time and were shouting and swearing about the service they were not getting; an officer came and told them to be quiet and wait their turn or they would be arrested. I had a little chuckle to myself and thought, "Some things never change!"

As I drove around the area that covered the six beats that my colleagues and I had patrolled all those years ago I hardly recognized any of it. The biggest difference, of course, is the end of the working docks. Areas like the Isle of Dogs are now almost entirely residential, with some of the warehouses now converted into expensive dockside dwellings. There are a few Chinese restaurants but Chinatown as I knew it has gone and most of the pubs have been pulled down, including Charlie Brown's. The one area that has not altered too much is Narrow Street in Wapping and I was delighted to find the Prospect of Whitby and the Town of Ramsgate pubs exactly as I remember them. I called in to the latter for half a pint and spent an interesting few minutes talking to one of the locals. When I told him why I'd come and that I was surprised how much Limehouse and the local population appeared to have changed, he agreed but said there are still a large number of true cockneys living in the area and he was proud to be one of them.

The final location I revisited was the road junction, described in the earlier chapter "Joining Division", that we knew as the Eastern Traffic Point. I did feel quite nostalgic as I stood and watched the traffic lights change at the very busy junction of Burdett East, Commercial Road, East India Dock Road and West India Dock Road and recalled the many hours my pals and I had stood in the middle of that junction getting filthy and breathing in the fumes from the traffic heading for the docks. I must admit that the traffic lights seemed to keep the traffic flowing a little bit more smoothly than we did, although we were good at sorting out snarl-ups — and causing them!

As I spent a couple of minutes reminiscing I noticed something that brought memories flooding back. I saw the very rundown-looking pub called the Star of the East still there in Commercial Road and it reminded me of an incident that took place in early 1962 when I hadn't long been at Limehouse. I was on Point Duty at the Eastern junction when a man shouted at me from the pavement and said a fight was taking place in the Star of the East public house. I left the middle of the road — and some confused drivers to sort themselves out as best they could — and went the few yards to the pub. When I entered there was indeed a fight taking place between two men but luckily none of the other customers were taking part in the fisticuffs. I shouted at the two combatants, who I guessed were dockers, to stop fighting and at that moment remembered what my mate Dave had told me on the first day I walked the beat with him, "Forget all that bollocks about 'What has happened here, Sir, please?' It won't work with a load of pissed-up dockers or sailors who are fighting, they'll tell you to fuck off."

That was very good advice, and I shouted at the men who were obviously drunk to pack it in immediately or I would get the landlord to phone for the cavalry and they would be arrested. I also told some of the other customers that if they were mates of the two they had best separate them and get them out of the pub. That all seemed to work and, despite the fact that both men were much bigger and stronger than me, they stopped fighting and left the pub with their mates without any further trouble. The landlord thanked me and offered me a quick drink, which I declined. I left the pub and returned to my Point Duty at the Eastern junction, which by that time, despite the fact that I had only been gone for about three minutes, was in absolute chaos, but it didn't take me long to sort out. Yes, despite my reservations about returning to Limehouse in 2013, that vivid memory made me glad that I did.

Acknowledgements

Thank you to my wife Anne and our children, who encouraged me to write this book, though goodness knows what my kids will think when they read what their dad was getting up to at a time when they thought all policemen were like PC Plod in their Noddy books!

Thank you to my good mate Nev Miles for his long friendship, encouragement and help in jogging my memory about some of the events I've written about. Also, special thanks go to my colleague John Bright, with whom I worked for several years. John, together with his wife Kath and their daughters, was a great friend to me and my family. John and Kath sadly passed away recently but I will never forget John's sense of humour — and dreadful jokes!

Many thanks to Louise Dixon, Senior Editorial Director (no relation to the author) for her professional help, support, patience and friendship. Also to George Maudsley, Jess Barratt, Emily Banyard and all at my publishers Michael O'Mara Books.

Finally, thanks to all those colleagues with whom I served and who were involved in some of the incidents I have described. If you recognize yourself in the stories, my solicitor is awaiting your call to remind you that everything in this book is true!

Other titles published by Ulverscroft:

THE BEST MEDICINE

Georgie Edwards

In 1949, Staff Nurse Georgie Edwards is asked to chaperone medical students undertaking their practical exams, when suddenly the penny drops. Georgie wants to learn to diagnose and treat, too. Against the odds, she wins herself a place to study medicine at London's St Bartholomew's Hospital. Once there, she sets about becoming not a consultant who 'sweeps by', but a doctor who listens and cares. Yet Georgie wants to fall in love and start a family as well as have a career. Is this one dream too many for a woman in the 1950s?

THE ZHIVAGO AFFAIR

Peter Finn & Petra Couvee

1956. Boris Pasternak knew his novel, *Doctor Zhivago*, would never be published in the Soviet Union as the authorities regarded it as seditious, so, instead, he pressed the manuscript into the hands of an Italian publishing scout and allowed it to be published in translation all over the world — a highly dangerous act.

1958. The CIA, recognising that the Cold War was primarily an ideological battle, published *Doctor Zhivago* in Russian and smuggled it into the Soviet Union. It was immediately snapped up on the black market. Pasternak was later forced to renounce the Nobel Prize in Literature, igniting worldwide political scandal.

With first access to previously classified CIA files, *The Zhivago Affair* gives an irresistible portrait of Pasternak, and takes us deep into the Cold War, back to a time when literature had the power to shake the world.

THE LAST BRITISH DAMBUSTER

George 'Johnny' Johnson

On 16 May 1943, Johnny Johnson, alongside 132 specially selected comrades, took off from Scampton airbase in Lincolnshire. For six weeks they had been trained to fulfil one mission that was near impossible: to destroy three dams deep within Germany's Ruhr Valley. It was a daring task but, against the odds, Johnny and his crew survived. Sadly, 53 comrades did not.

For the first time, Johnny relives every moment of that fatal night — and the devastating aftermath. He recalls with unique wit and insight the difficult training conducted in secrecy, the race against time to release the bombs, and the sheer strength and bravery shown by a small unit faced with great adversity and uncertainty. Embodying a whole squadron, and leaving a lasting legacy for generations to come, Johnny's story is like no other.

A CURIOUS CAREER

Lynn Barber

A Curious Career takes us from Lynn's early years as a journalist at Penthouse to her later more eminent role interrogating a huge cross-section of celebrities. It is full of glorious anecdotes — the interview with Salvador Dali that ended up lasting four days, or the drinking session with Shane MacGowan. It also contains eye-opening transcripts, such as her infamous interview with the hilarious and spectacularly rude Marianne Faithfull. A wonderfully frank and funny memoir by Britain's greatest and most ferocious interviewer, *A Curious Career* is also a fascinating window into the lives of celebrities and the changing world of journalism.